The Natural History of a Royal Forest

David Steel

Illustrated by Barbara Cooper & Peter Creed

Pisces
PUBLICATIONS

First published 1984 by Pisces Publications, Brasenose Farm, Eastern By-pass, Oxford.
Hardback ISBN 0-9508245-2-6
Paperback ISBN 0-9508245-1-8

Designed by Pisces Publications

Printed by Holywell Press, Alfred Street, Oxford

British Library Cataloguing in Publication Data

Steel, D.T.
  The Natural History of a Royal Forest.
  1. Natural history — England — Shotover Forest
  I. Title
  508.425′79   QH138.S5

  ISBN 0-9508245-2-6
  ISBN 0-9508245-1-8 Pbk

Contents

Introduction

Shotover was one of England's smaller royal forests. Since the loss of royal forest status in the seventeenth century it has become so fragmented as to become hardly recognizable as a forest. Partly because of its proximity to Oxford many documents are available which give us an insight into what went on in the forest, and enable us to follow the fate of the forest in more recent years. It is particularly revealing to interpret present day natural history features in terms of their royal forest history.

The name Shotover is mentioned in the Domesday book, the entry reading

'*In Scotorne . . . dñice foreftae regis*',

[in Shotover are the lordship forests of the king[1]]. One local legend suggests that the name Shotover comes from a time when two giants lived on either side of the hill and 'shot' large stones 'over' the hill at each other. Another story has it that Robin Hood or Oliver Cromwell 'shot' arrows 'over' the hill[12]. Another legend suggests that the name is derived from *Chateau vert* referring to a green hunting lodge on the north side of the hill. However, etymologists believe the most likely derivation is from the Old English *sceot ofer*, which means steep hill[35].

The core of Shotover Royal Forest was on the sandstone hill to the east of Oxford – the highest of the hills surrounding Oxford. 125 ha of the south side of the hill are now occupied by Shotover Country Park which with its woodland, scrub and grassland, must bear some resemblance to its appearance in royal forest times. Much of the rest of the royal forest area has been converted to arable farming, and the remaining comparatively untouched areas of woodland and pasture are few and far between.

Dramatic changes have taken place in Oxfordshire's countryside since medieval times and some of these changes are still continuing. Because of its former status as a royal forest we are able to map with some accuracy the changes which have occurred at Shotover. An understanding of the changes which have taken place turn our thoughts to the future. Do we want the surviving fragments of royal forest to remain or should we allow their loss to continue?

Acknowledgements

Many people have provided valuable assistance in the gathering of information for this book. G. Bloom, H.J.M. Bowen, J. Buchanan, P. Creed, J.P. Dear, R.H.L. Disney, J. Facey, C. Gibson, A. Hill, E.W. Jones, L. Losito, R. Louch, I. McLean, S. Marner, N. Mills, D. Newman, D. Owen, G. Philpott, J. Pitts, A. Stubbs, R. Tapper, J. Tyler, P. Waring and M. Warland all provided records of one sort or another as did BBONT and the Nature Conservancy Council.

A valuable section on Hymenoptera was written by C. O'Toole, and a translation from the Latin of a 1298 perambulation made by E. Black. The arduous task of typing all drafts was accomplished by Mrs Gwenneth Steel. Dr. R. Hornby and N. Ajax-Lewis read and made valuable comments on the

Introduction

text. Thanks must go to J.R.J. Advertising of Wantage for their support and financial assistance.

   I would like to thank Peter Creed and Barbie Cooper for providing excellent illustrations and organizing the layout of the production. My wife Caroline provided important assistance in numerous ways. The photographs are by Henry Taunt (p 20) courtesy of Oxfordshire County Libraries, Peter Creed (back cover, p 71), B.A.C. Peart (pp 32, 33, 40, 60, 62, 67, 68) and David Steel (pp 26, 28, 29, 36, 39, 42, 45, 46, 50, 55, 57, 65, 74, 75).

David Steel
Oxford, December 1983

Chapter 1

History of Shotover Forest

Prehistoric Shotover

Present day Shotover is very different from the natural forest which it replaced. No direct evidence about the nature of this forest is available, but it is possible to make some tentative assertions based on evidence from other parts of Britain and Europe. Following the Pleistocene glaciation Oxfordshire became extremely well wooded and these forests may have contained animals such as elk, reindeer and auroch (wild ox), remains of which have been found in northern Britain where they became extinct long before the Anglo-Saxon period. Animals which may have been found at Shotover at the time of the Roman occupation include wolf, wild cat and brown bear. Wolves were common during the Anglo-Saxon period. Wild cats, which still survive in Scotland, were formerly common throughout Britain disappearing only when woodland was cleared for cultivation. A wild cat is said to have been caught in Holton Wood in 1863 [2]. It was said to have been

> 'a genuine and splendid wild cat which looked like a small tiger and was 31½" long and weighed 9¾lb.'

However, this was probably a feral cat rather than a true wild cat. The question of brown bears is more problematical, but they were found in northern England until the tenth century and as their present day habitat in Europe is deciduous woodland, they may have existed in Oxfordshire at an early date.

Other animals present in prehistoric Shotover include red deer, roe deer and wild boar, but these did not disappear until comparatively recent times. Red deer were still present in Wychwood Forest until 1856 [3] and their hides were used by the glove manufacturing industry at Chipping Norton. It is likely that both red and roe deer were still to be found at Shotover in Medieval times. Wild boar hunting was a favourite pastime of Norman kings. Boars are known to have been in Wychwood Forest in the thirteenth century when Henry III instructed two boars to be taken from Wychwood to Havering, which was part of Waltham Forest [4]. There is an interesting legend concerning wild boars at Shotover whereby a student of the Queen's College named Copcot, was walking in Shotover Forest reading Aristotle when a boar attacked him. The student rammed the volume down the throat of the beast saying the words

> 'Graecum est'

and the boar expired. This episode is remembered by an oil painting in the Queen's College, a stained-glass window in Horspath church and an annual ceremony in the Queen's College where a boar's head, with an orange between its teeth, is carried aloft in procession into Hall every Christmas Day. The family crest of the Tyrell family, who lived in Shotover House in the seventeenth century, was a boar's head with a peacock feather in its mouth. The boar's head story can only be a legend because Greek was not taught at Oxford University at this time. However, one element of the story which makes it more believable is that Copcot is a local name, being derived from a place name near Tetsworth. It is certain that wild boar were present in prehistoric Shotover but they probably became extinct in the forest during Anglo-Saxon times.

The vegetation of Shotover would have been largely high forest with oaks predominating. The pedunculate oak is the most abundant tree at Shotover now but it is possible that the sessile oak was more widespread in natural forest. Subsequent planting favoured the pedunculate oak which was thought to be the better timber tree. Although oaks were the most abundant tree, there were lesser numbers of other species such as silver birch, field maple, aspen, wild cherry and wild service tree. Apart from conifers the only alien tree species present in any numbers at Shotover is the sycamore, which was introduced to England as an ornamental in Tudor times. One tree species which may have been present in natural Oxfordshire forest but which is now absent from Shotover is the small-leaved lime (*Tilia cordata*). Pollen analysis of lime shows that it was widespread in England 5 – 7,500 years ago[60].

We have no evidence concerning herbaceous plants found in natural Oxfordshire wildwood but it is likely that it contained many species still present. A striking feature of wildwood is the amount of dead and fallen

timber present – recent measurements from natural deciduous forest in Poland show that about as much wood is decaying on the ground as is standing – a marked contrast to the tidy, managed woodland of today.

The first direct evidence of human habitation at Shotover comes from the finding of flint chips, flakes, scrapers and arrow heads produced by a flint knapper in Neolithic times and found at several places including the vicinity of Westhill Farm [5]. The nearest flint sources to Shotover are the Chilterns and Berkshire Downs and so any flint found at Shotover must have been brought from a distance. Two long barrows existed at the western end of Shotover Plain until their destruction by military activity during the Second World War. It is thought that a prehistoric route existed between Dorchester and Oxford along the line of the future Roman road [3], and it is not surprising that such a well-drained and easily defended site as Shotover Hill was settled by early man.

Roman Shotover

Oxford was not heavily settled in Roman times but it was a major centre for the production of pottery [6]. Shotover Hill is just to the north of the Roman road between Dorchester and Alchester. Many kiln sites have been found near this road including one on Shotover Hill (in Row field to the east of Shotover Plain), one in Open Brasenose (discovered as recently as 1969) and others at Woodeaton, Headington Wick and the Churchill Hospital – all within the bounds of what became Shotover Royal Forest. The Shotover kilns produced colour-coated wares, parchment wares, white wares and mortaria. Suitable clay for the grey and red wares could have come from either Kimmeridge or Oxford clays, but the white wares depend on iron-free clays of which Shotover had the only considerable source in its Wealden beds. This white clay was used for pipe-making until the seventeenth century. The Shotover kilns were in operation from 240 – 400 A.D. and the white ware mortaria from Open Brasenose have been found all over Oxfordshire.

The presence of these kilns would certainly have had a considerable influence on Shotover Forest. The kilns would have been fuelled with local wood, and oaks from around the kilns would have been felled for this purpose. The Romans are known to have introduced certain plant and animal species to Britain, some of which are still found at Shotover. Henbane and ground-elder are two plants said to have been introduced for their medicinal value. Ground-elder is common near habitation at Shotover. Henbane is not common but it did appear in profusion near Open Brasenose in 1976 and it may be that the hot dry summer of 1975 broke dormancy and allowed existing seeds to germinate. Fallow deer, possibly introduced by the Romans, were an important constituent of the medieval Royal Forest.

To sum up, Shotover Hill was well known to the Romans, particularly as a source of iron-free clays. Although the Romans felled many trees for fuel and building, it is likely that these areas rapidly reverted to forest after the

Romans left. The most lasting influence of the Romans was through the plant and animal species which they introduced.

Shotover Royal Forest

Royal forests were established in Saxon times and forest laws are known to have existed in the time of King Canute (c. 995 – 1035). These forests were areas of land, part woodland and part pasture, subject to strict laws exercised by a complicated system of courts and officials. The earliest surviving written regulation dealing with forest laws is the Assize of Woodstock (1184), but this embodied earlier customs and legal practice. Royal forests had something of a chequered history, with monarchs such as Henry II increasing the area of land subject to forest laws (afforestation) while others, such as Edward I, reduced the area subject to forest laws (disafforestation). However, neither afforestation nor disafforestation involved felling or planting of trees.

Land subject to forest law was not necessarily owned by the Crown. In Domesday, Shotover is described as one of the King's 'demesne' forests which suggests that it was owned by the monarch. However, by the thirteenth century it is documented that certain religious houses owned parcels of land within the forest and for most of its history several land owners were involved at Shotover.

The early boundary of Shotover can be gleaned from a perambulation (a boundary survey), undertaken in about 1298, a translation of which is included in Appendix 1. This boundary is shown on Fig. 1 superimposed on a present day parish boundary map. Most of this boundary interpretation is based on a study by Roberts[8]. The area of Shotover Royal Forest at this time was approximately 2,300 ha. Also shown on Fig. 1 are woodlands, formerly within the forest, which were disafforested by Edward I. For comparison the boundary of Shotover Forest in 1643[9], seventeen years before disafforestation, is shown (Fig. 2) and it can be seen that the area subject to forest laws had shrunk to about 600 ha by that time.

The best known function of royal forests was to provide hunting facilities exclusively for the king. However, no records of any monarchs visiting Shotover are available even though they are known to have frequently visited neighbouring Wychwood Forest and Woodstock Chase. Shotover itself lay beside the route from Westminster to the Royal Manor of Woodstock and so every monarch would have passed Shotover and it is almost certain that all monarchs would have hunted there. The reason no records are available is that such an event would not have been considered newsworthy. It is probable that more important functions of royal forests were in raising revenue through sales and forest courts, and as perquisites to favoured individuals and organizations.

It is known that the king's table at Windsor was sometimes replenished with venison from Shotover[10]. In 1613 the baliwick of Shotover was granted to Sir Timothy Tyrell. There is a tradition that the reason for this

Fig. 1   The boundary of Shotover Royal Forest in 1298

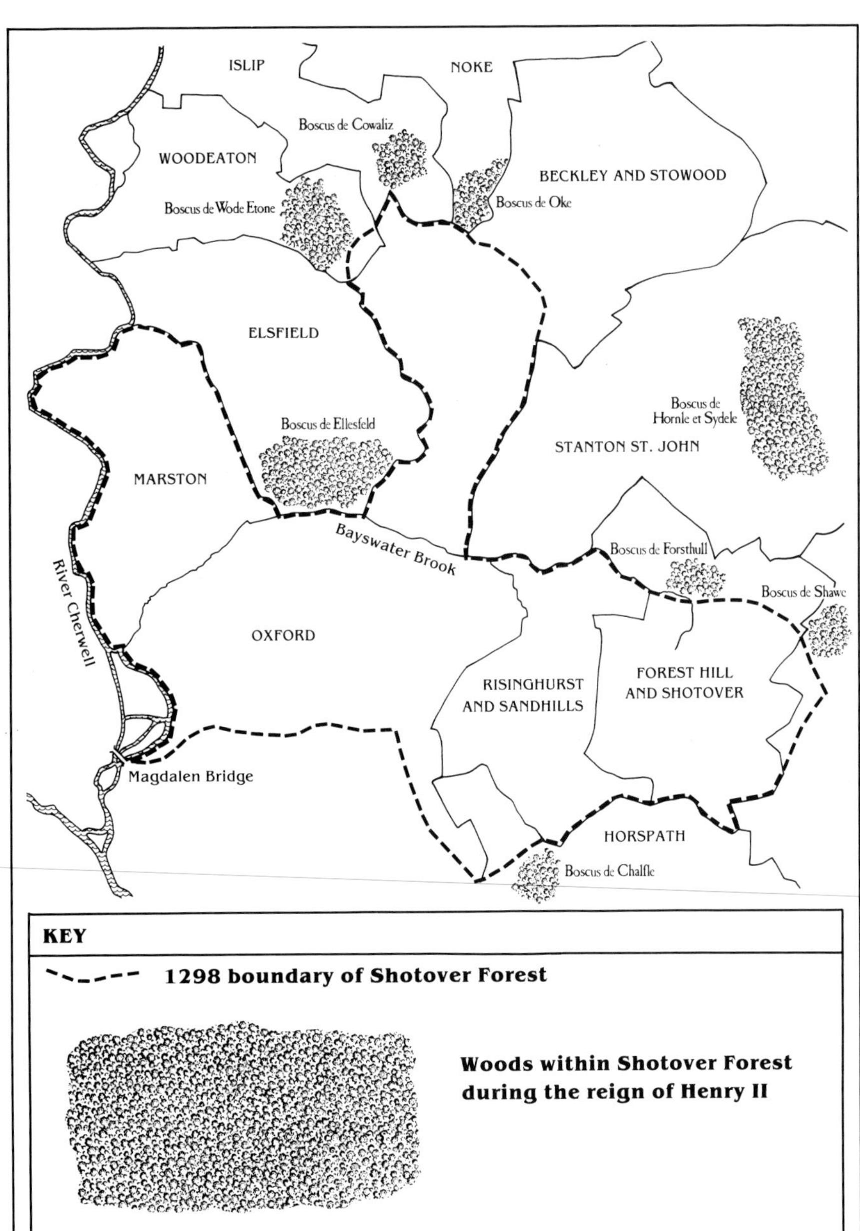

KEY

- – – – – – **1298 boundary of Shotover Forest**

Woods within Shotover Forest during the reign of Henry II

Fig. 2   The boundary of Shotover Royal Forest in 1642

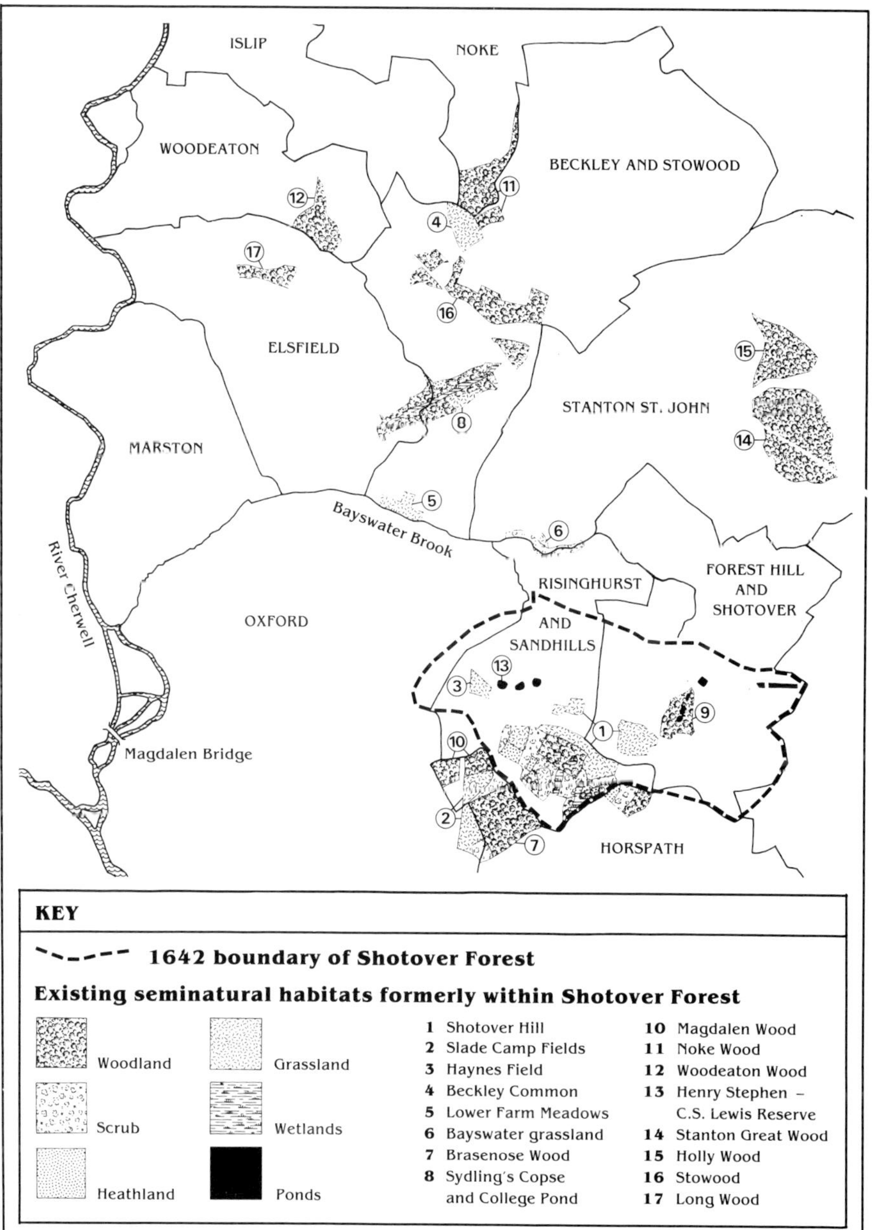

KEY

- - - - -   1642 boundary of Shotover Forest

Existing seminatural habitats formerly within Shotover Forest

Woodland

Grassland

Scrub

Wetlands

Heathland

Ponds

1   Shotover Hill
2   Slade Camp Fields
3   Haynes Field
4   Beckley Common
5   Lower Farm Meadows
6   Bayswater grassland
7   Brasenose Wood
8   Sydling's Copse
    and College Pond

10   Magdalen Wood
11   Noke Wood
12   Woodeaton Wood
13   Henry Stephen –
     C.S. Lewis Reserve
14   Stanton Great Wood
15   Holly Wood
16   Stowood
17   Long Wood

gift was that while hunting with the Prince of Wales, Sir Timothy held a buck's head for the Prince to sever. The Prince's blow badly wounded Sir Timothy's hand and the baliwick of Shotover was by way of compensation for the injury. However, it is not certain that this incident, if it happened at all, took place at Shotover.

Local forest courts or *Swainmotes* are known to have taken place at Shotover at least from the thirteenth to the seventeenth century, but the only court about which any details are extant was held at Headington on 9 June 1636[11]. This is a late date in the history of royal forests and in many places forest laws had begun to decay before this time. During the reign of Charles I there was an attempt to revive strict forest jurisdiction. This example gives an insight into the hierarchy of forest officers as well as the range of offences committed. All the forest officers were present. Henry Lord Holland was keeper, the chief local authority of the forest and a post which carried many perquisites and privileges. Sir Henry Cooke and Mr Unton Croke were the two verderers, elected by freeholders in the county court and whose duties were concerned with the forest courts. Three foresters were present each of which was in charge of a 'walk' within the forest, namely New Lodge Walk, Old Lodge Walk and Stowood. Edward Whistler was woodward for the whole forest and his duties included ensuring that the underwood was properly enclosed before the coppice was cut, paying labourers employed in fence making, dividing underwood into lots for sale, directing any tree felling and making sure that any person trespassing within the forest was brought to justice. Twelve regarders were present and these men, originally knights, made a triannual inspection of the forest and reported to the forest courts. Two gentlemen keepers were at the court whose duties involved looking after the forest deer. Two agisters were present whose duties were to oversee any grazing within the forest. Cattle, sheep and swine were all grazed in the forest and payments (agistments) were collected for this privilege. Other forest officers present at the court were five sub-foresters, two wardens and two pages. As can be seen a considerable number of officers and labourers were employed in various activities within the forest.

Offences in the forest come under four headings: venison (killing deer or wild boar), vert (damaging timber or underwood), assart (enclosing land within the forest) and purpresture (building within the forest). At this 1636 court Roger Gardiner was fined £100 for killing two bucks and two does. John Symondes of Headington was fined £5 for killing does with a 'moungrell' dog. John Weston was fined £20 for netting hares and William Willoughby was fined £10 for catching a fawn in a saw pit. As an example of an offence against vert William Willoughby, a shipwright, was fined £2,020 for felling fifty oaks valued at 20s each and grubbing up their roots valued at 5s each. Other delinquents were fined £5 for removing an ash worth 3s, £2 for removing an ash worth 6d and £10 for taking 3 cartloads of ash worth 20s. As can be imagined these fines were extremely severe but they do not compare with the mutilation and death meted out by the courts in Norman times. The Anglo-Saxon chronicle for 1087 states that

King William legislated that

> *'Whosoever should slay hart or hind should be blinded.'*

Other sources of revenue to the Crown and forest officers included the sale of timber and underwood, and the collection of agistments for animals pastured within the forest. Timber from Shotover was used in the construction of many buildings including Oxford gaol[11], Oxford and Wallingford Castles, Chapel of St. Mary in the Hospice of St. John the Baptist and the Bodleian Library[12]. Even though Shotover is far from the coast its oaks were valued for shipbuilding. In 1629 shipwrights visited Shotover and censused over 27,000 trees which they wanted for their own use stating that the oaks were

> *'the best in the kingdome for shippinge, both for hardness and toughnesse thereof being not apt to rend or cleave'*[13]

Studley Priory was granted the right to sell underwood from a wood within the forest[14]. Villages with no common grazing paid agistment to the swainmote for the right to pasture animals within the forest. In 1363 Noke sent 12 pigs, Islip 20 pigs, Woodeaton 6 pigs, Elsfield 8 pigs, Beckley 10 pigs, Forest Hill 12 pigs, Wheatley 10 pigs, Horspath 18 pigs and Cowley 10 pigs into the forest at the rate of 1s6d per pig, part of the fee going to the Crown and part to the senior forest officers[7]. The pigs were only allowed in the forest during the pannage (acorn eating) season lasting from 14 September until 18 November (21 September to 25 November in the modern calendar). In 1452 agistments totalled 28s7¾d plus eighteen bushels of wheat. Other minor sources of revenue included cokshotes (payments of hens and eggs for the privilege of collecting dry wood within

the forest) and chiminage which was payment for the right of driving beasts through the forest.

A final source of revenue was the payments made for quarrying within the forest. White clay for pipemaking was quarried until the seventeenth century. Ochre, said by Robert Plot to be the finest in the kingdom[15], was quarried for many centuries. The poor quality ochre was used as a dye for painting waggons: traditionally the body of Oxfordshire waggons was yellow but the wheels and bed were red[31]. The finest quality ochre was used for paint pigments and was ground at a mill near Wheatley. The Cuddesdon Charter of 956 was the first endowment of St. Ethelwold's reconstituted Abingdon Abbey. In the famous Benedictional of St. Ethelwold, which was once kept at Chatsworth and is now stored in the National Library, the animal on which Christ is entering Jerusalem is painted with mineral ochre, which may have been from Shotover as a good and local source[2].

Many individuals and organizations (religious houses in particular) benefited from gifts and favours and some of these had an important influence on the later history of the forest. Gifts of venison were frequent: in 1278 four bucks were sent from Shotover as a gift to Bartholomew de Sutlegh and in 1281 six bucks were sent to James de Ispannia, nephew of Queen Eleanor the King's Consort[11]. The Knight's Templars, who owned a wood to the south east of the present day Brasenose Wood, were granted the right to take ten bucks annually. Certain organizations were excused payments of pannage and were allowed to herd swine free of charge. In 1443, Humphrey Duke of Gloucester, keeper of the royal forests to the south of the river Trent, granted the Hospice of St John the Baptist the

right to put fifty pigs in Whittlewood Forest, fifty in Bernwood and fifty in Shotover free of pannage[16].

Gifts of underwood were common and in later years these were sometimes superseded by gifts of land. In 1222 Henry III granted the brethren of the Hospital of St. Bartholomew the right to gather one hundred bundles of dead wood for burning from Shotover. In 1234 the Hospice of St John the Baptist, on whose site Magdalen College now stands, was granted the right to collect a load of wood for fuel by sumpter horse twice daily from the forest. In 1246 this right was replaced by a gift of land within the forest, which was later known as Wood Farm and included Magdalen Wood[51].

In 1226 Henry III granted the Prioress of Littlemore the right to take a sumpter horse twice daily into the forest to collect dead wood and thorn for fuel[34]. This concession was replaced in 1259 by a gift of 27 acres of forest. The location of this gift is given as being bounded by the wood of the Templars (probably Peryhale which is now an arable field to the S.E. of Brasenose Common), the King's Wood (Shotover to the north) and Wodewardesmede (later Wood Farm). Brasenose Wood has an earth bank running S.W. to N.E. which divides the wood into two and as the parcel of woodland to the north of the mound measures 27.59 acres, it is possible that this is the same woodland granted to the prioress in the thirteenth century. While in the possession of the Prioress of Littlemore the wood was known as Minchery Wood. This name was derived from the obsolete word minchin which in turn came from the Old English *mynecenu* meaning nun[35]. Minchery Wood was later increased in size to about 80 acres to include all of Brasenose Wood and Open Brasenose.

In 1569 Sir Christopher Brome purchased 'Myncherye Woodde' from Edmund Powell of Lampeforde for £40[36]. In 1579 Brasenose College obtained Minchery Woods from Sir Christopher Brome by means of a swap with land at Forest Hill and Northam and Bradmore[37]. Records in the archives of Brasenose College show that the wood was being actively coppiced during the sixteenth century. In 1570 Elizabeth I granted the College the right to continue

> *'laying waste, rearranging and repairing their 80 acre coppice in Heddendon'*[38]

Brasenose College managed the woodland by letting it on a series of 21 year leases. For example in 1654 the woods were let to Wm. Combes for £22[39]. Conditions of the lease provided that the tenant was to

> *'repair, cleanse, and scour the ditches, hedges, fences, mounds and watercourses in the woods and to surrender all in good condition'.*

An extra payment of £5 was to be made for every acre of land ploughed up or 'eased'. It is interesting to note that Wm. Combes recovered a good deal of his rent back from the College on payment for timber for building in the College. For example in 1656 there is an entry in the Account Book

> *'payd to Wm. Combes for 3 sapling oaks counting 84' at 15½d per foot = £5.8.6 for laths for chapple'*[40]

The system of 21 year leases was continued into the early years of the twentieth century.

The presence of a royal forest would have had great local significance, both as a source of revenue to the forest officers and some local organizations, and as a restriction on local peasants some of whom frequently infringed the forest laws. The forest was managed with the aim of maintaining a good stock of deer, maintaining the timber and underwood in a healthy condition and producing revenue from grazing the forest pasture. In order to achieve these aims a high level of activity was necessary and many people were employed in the forest.

Decline of Shotover Forest

During the period when Sir Timothy Tyrell was Keeper of Shotover Forest (1613 – 60) the woods decayed leading to disafforestation in 1660. There were significant demands for timber from the navy at this time because the New Forest and Forest of Dean had been worked out. Further demands on Shotover's timber came from the works on the banks of the river Thames. Sir Timothy is said to have unnecessarily felled many oaks and it is also said that the revenue from timber sales went into the pocket of the forest officers rather than the Crown. This period of waste and decay was compounded during the period of the Civil War when Oxford was the capital of the Royalists. During the siege of Oxford much of Shotover's wood was used for fuel and some of the larger trunks were used for fortification. Finally in 1660, in the reign of Charles II, Shotover was shown to be in such poor condition that it was disafforested or made no longer subject to forest laws. After disafforestation those with rights of common were compensated by gifts of land (641 acres), while the rest (983 acres) was leased by the Crown, the lessees being encouraged to build and plough. The estate was purchased from the Crown in 1745 by Augustus Schutz, and is still largely in private hands although three farms (Westhill Farm, Wood Farm and Brasenose Farm) were acquired by Oxford City Council in the first half of the twentieth century.

Throughout the period of Shotover Royal Forest the main route from Oxford to London passed over Shotover Hill. The occupants of the coach were obliged to dismount and walk up the steepest sections. There is a record of a Dutch scholar named Mathew Slade expiring due to the rigours of the uphill walk in December 1689[17]. A stone used for remounting the coach is still to be found at the western end of Shotover Plain.

The area to either side of Shotover Plain was a wild and desolate place and there are several records of dastardly deeds. One of the most famous victims of highway robbery was Charles Wesley[57], who one October day in 1739 was travelling from Oxford to London on horseback. He had not gone more than a mile from the city when his mount went lame. So, as is recorded, he commended himself to Divine protection and began to sing the 91st Psalm, that robust anthem which assures the believer that the

Almighty will deliver him from 'the snare of the hunter', 'the noisome pestilence', 'terror by night' and 'the arrow that flieth by day', among a long catalogue of perils with which the righteous are bound to be assailed.

The traveller had hardly ended the singing, and had but that moment passed the hut on Shotover Hill (presumably Titup Hall, now the Crown and Thistle) when a man came up and asked him for his money. The highwayman showed no pistol, but Charles Wesley handed over his purse containing thirty shillings. 'Have you no more?' asked the robber, whereupon he put his hand in his pocket and gave the man some halfpence.

Again the highwayman asked the question. Now Charles Wesley could not tell a lie so he bade the fellow search for himself. It was a successful ruse for the highwayman, evidently never before having met a traveller not prepared to lie with fluency and a good conscience, took the rejoinder as a surly way of saying 'no' and did not search him. Wesley salved his conscience and saved the thirty guineas he had in another pocket.

In the 12 January 1760 edition of Jackson's Oxford Journal it is recorded that

> 'Last Saturday morning the Birmingham stage was robbed about five o'clock in the morning at Shotover Hill, near this city, by two young fellows, in blue close-bodied coats, mounted on black horses; they took from the passengers about seventeen pounds and after giving the coachman and postilion a shilling each, rode off.'

In the 9 September 1773 edition it is recorded that

> 'Last Saturday morning Mr Way of Thame in this county was stopped in the Hollow Way on the side of Shotover Hill facing Wheatley by two footpads in carter's smock frocks one of whom seized his horse's bridle, and immediately brandished a bludgeon whilst the other brandished a pistol which he clapped to Mr Way's chest and he threatened to shoot him dead if he did not instantly deliver his money; upon which Mr Way desired him to remove his pistol and he would give it him; the fellow did so and received a purse containing twenty six pounds five shilllngs and sixpence, with which they both went off contented, wishing him a good night'.

In the last quarter of the eighteenth century the Stokenchurch Turnpike was completed (later to become the present A40) and the need to cross Shotover Hill removed.

Chapter 2

Natural History

When subject to forest law Shotover Royal Forest was covered almost entirely by seminatural vegetation, although the 1298 perambulation shows that there was some arable land within the forest. The forest was not truly natural because many of man's activities had an influence on the nature of the vegetation. However, very little intensive management occurred, and so the plant communities found were strongly related to those which would be present if the area were uninhabited by man. The fate of Shotover's seminatural vegetation is of particular interest because it contains a rich assemblage of native plants and animals. Indeed, many species are so closely adapted to life in a seminatural community that they are quite unable to survive outside it.

During the reign of Edward I Shotover Royal Forest was at least 3,000 ha in extent. By 1298 the area subject to forest laws had diminished to about 2,300 ha. At disafforestation in 1660 the area of the Royal Forest was only 600 ha. A detailed survey of the surviving seminatural remnants of the forest (see Table 1) shows that only about 252 ha remain, thus representing about 8.4% of the area of the original Shotover Royal Forest. It is interesting to note that about 140 ha of seminatural woodland remain, compared to 58.6 ha of seminatural grassland, 3.5 ha of heath and 5.0 ha of fen and marsh.

There are many reasons for the dramatic loss of seminatural vegetation. Some woods were felled during the royal forest period. For instance, we can deduce that Peryhale, a wood at one time owned by the Knight's Templars and situated to the S.E. of Open Brasenose, was felled prior to 1605 when it is shown as agricultural land on a map of Corpus Christi college lands drawn by Thomas Langdon[18]. In the seventeenth century many trees were requisitioned by the navy's shipwrights and transported to the coast[13]. Considerable tree felling took place near Oxford at the time of the civil war for purposes of fuel and fortification[20]. Much woodland was felled or 'eased' following disafforestation. In 1852 – 53 ten acres of Brasenose Wood were felled and converted to arable usage[19]. Upper Horley or Gogmire Wood, which was formerly a northerly extension of the present day Holly Wood, was felled between 1856 and the early years of the twentieth century[20]. Woodeaton Wood is known to have been 96.5 acres in 1366 but only 34 acres in 1881[8]. As recently as 1981 a strip of ancient woodland close to Stowood was felled and converted to arable.

In the twentieth century a substantial area of ancient woodland was felled and converted to coniferous plantation. Stowood formerly possessed a rich and diverse flora. Druce, writing in the 1930s[3], states that

> 'in Stowood . . . there are expanses of dog's mercury, columbine, meadow saxifrage and nettle-leaved bellflower'.

Table 1   Remaining seminatural habitat within the bounds of the former Shotover Royal Forest.

Grassland	Shotover Hill(acid grassland) Slade camp fields Haynes field Beckley Common Lower Farm Meadows Sydling's Copse Bayswater	18.00ha 15.80ha 5.80ha 2.00ha 15.00ha 1.50ha 0.50ha ———— 58.60ha
Scrub	Shotover Hill Brasenose Wood edge Bayswater Brook Valley Sydling's Copse	23.00ha 5.00ha 10.00ha 3.00ha ———— 42.00ha
Heath	Shotover Hill Sydling's Copse	3.00ha 0.50ha ———— 3.50ha
Woodland	Johnson's Piece Magdalen Wood Brasenose Wood Sydling's and Wick Copse Stowood Woodeaton Wood Noke Wood Long Wood Holly Wood Stanton Great Wood	18.19ha 4.25ha 18.37ha 8.00ha(+ 2.00ha conifers) 5.00ha(+ 21.50ha conifers) 15.00ha 23.00ha(+ 4.00ha conifers) 6.00ha 12.00ha(+ 1.00ha conifers) 30.00ha(+ 30.00ha conifers) ———— 139.81ha
Freshwater ponds and streams	Henry Stephen / C.S. Lewis ponds Shotover Spinney ponds Shotover House ponds	1.00ha 1.00ha 2.00ha ———— 4.00ha
Wetland	Sydling's Copse fen Shotover Hill marsh	3.00ha 2.00ha ———— 5.00ha

Most figures in the above Table are approximate.

Expanses of dog's mercury are still found under the peripheral hazel coppice but the other species are gone. The main body of the wood was felled and replanted with conifers during the Second World War. Sydling's Copse, Shotover Spinney, Stanton Great Wood and Noke Wood all have substantial conifer plantations.

For most of their lifespan conifer plantations cast a dense shade which allows a very poor ground flora. There are some compensations – conifer plantations support many nesting birds including the uncommon firecrest. Several uncommon insects seem to prefer this habitat. However, there is no doubt that on balance the coniferisation of ancient woodland is detrimental to nature conservation interests.

The loss of seminatural heathland is less well documented but Druce writes in the early years of this century[3]

> *'The once celebrated district of Shotover has suffered much during the last century, at the beginning of which it was open and uncultivated ground, in parts thickly wooded and in others showing delightful expanses of heath . . . The inclosure of the heathy slopes, the cultivation of its surface . . . have gradually denuded the hill of its characteristic vegetation and the process of destruction still goes on'.*

Comparison of the view of Shotover Hill from Cowley Barracks by the renowned Oxford photographer Henry Taunt in 1880 with the same view today, shows how the processes of inclosure and cultivation have continued. In the 1920s many hectares of heathland to the south side of Shotover Hill were lost. 2.5 ha were planted with European larch and about 15 ha were used for low density housing with the heathland being trans-

View of Shotover Hill from near Cowley Barracks (1880)

formed into domestic gardens. A photograph of a newly constructed thatched cottage designed by Thomas Rayson appeared in the April 1921 issue of Homes and Gardens and clearly shows open heathland in the background[21].

Since 1930 Shotover's heathland has declined in quantity and quality because of the lack of human interference! This apparent paradox results from the fact that heathland has to be maintained by grazing or burning. These activities ceased at Shotover and the result was the encroachment of woody plants and dense stands of bracken, and the subsequent demise of the varied heath flora. The only other surviving remnant of heathland is immediately to the north of Sydling's Copse. This remnant is dominated by bracken and has survived several abortive attempts by the tenant farmer to convert to arable usage.

Seminatural grassland has been lost both to the plough and to 'agricultural improvements' such as reseeding or treatment with fertilizers and pesticides. Little documentation is available on the loss of unimproved grassland but we know, for example, that in 1949 there was a substantial area of unimproved, limestone grassland to the north of Bayswater Brook. Butterflies such as chalkhill blue and small blue abounded here and the flowery grassland contained plants such as clustered bellflower, squinancy wort and autumn gentian. This grassland was ploughed at some time between 1949 and 1972. 'Agricultural improvements' by fertilizer application and reseeding have taken place in the early 1980s on some of the acidic grasslands to the north of Shotover Hill. Changes wrought by such practices are less dramatic than those caused by ploughing but the resulting loss of native species is no less profound.

The natural history of arable fields, an artificial habitat, has declined over the past 200 years. Thorow-wax (*Bupleurum rotundifolium*), corncockle (*Agrostemma githago*), corn buttercup (*Ranunculus arvensis*), rough poppy (*Papaver hybridum*) and corn parsley (*Petroselinum segetum*) are documented examples of extinctions. Some arable field bryophytes are known to have been lost, and others such as *Acaulon muticum* only remain in minute quantities. Losses are continuing – cornflower (*Centaurea cyanus*) grew near Sydling's Copse until 1981. Some unusual weeds remain – the tiny venus's looking-glass (*Legousia hybrida*), many-seeded goosefoot (*Chenopodium polyspermum*) and the beautiful corn marigold (*Chrysanthemum segetum*) are still found but each year in diminishing quantities. The reason for these changes is that improvements in agricultural practice result in purer seed corn and increased use of herbicides.

The vegetation of Shotover has changed dramatically since royal forest times. The diminution of seminatural vegetation has reduced the number of places suitable for many of our native plants and animals. Not all changes have been harmful – the construction of ponds on the Shotover Estate and the more recent clay pit ponds at Risinghurst, have provided valuable freshwater habitats. However, most changes have been harmful and have resulted in the loss and fragmentation of much valuable wildlife habitat.

Chapter 3

The Geology of Shotover

Shotover Hill stands, at 171 metres, as the highest of the hills surrounding Oxford. Shotover is a steep-sided but flat topped hill, with flat bottomed valleys to the north and south. The Shotover Sands which cap the hill are porous and comparatively resistant to erosion – such flat topped hills are a feature of wherever ironsands are exposed. Forest Hill is a small outlier capped with Shotover Sands.

A geological map (Fig. 3) shows that the oldest rocks outcropping at Shotover are the dark, Oxford clays which form a belt of low country stretching from north Wiltshire to Peterborough. These clays were deposited at the bottom of a deep sea which then covered Oxfordshire. As this upper Jurassic sea became shallower, alterations took place in the type of deposit laid down, with a change from clays to sands (calcareous grit) and then to shallow water limestone (Coral Rag). However, the youngest Coral Rag rocks contain a mixture of clays, sandstones and limestones. Above the Coral Rag is a 22 – 24 metres thick bed of Kimmeridge rocks, mostly grey and black clays laid down at the bottom of a deep sea about 150 million years ago. The youngest Kimmeridge beds are the five metres thick Shotover Grit Sands containing doggers (concretionary masses of sandstone often of great size) which are exposed in several places at Shotover. Doggers are formed by gradual deposition of quartz around a nucleus but there are several local legends concerning the origin and purpose of doggers. In the twelfth century Empress Matilda, the enemy of King Stephen, was staying in London when a change of allegiance within the army put her life in danger. She immediately travelled to Oxford where safety was to be found. On reaching Shotover Hill Matilda expressed her relief by bursting into tears and it is said that her tears were so voluminous that as they fell they hardened into enormous boulders now seen as doggers. Doggers are also known as 'Giant's Marbles' and there are several different legends concerning giants at Shotover, which may date back to the seventeenth century when a figure of a giant was cut into the hillside[22]. An unusually shaped dogger, known locally as 'Giant's Loaf', was formerly found at the junction of the Ridings and the Old Road up to Shotover Hill.

Above the Kimmeridge beds are the Portland sands and limestones which were deposited near the edge of a shallow sea. The youngest and oldest Portland beds are limestones but the biggest outcrop is the Middle Portland, made up of mustard coloured sands with occasional concretionary masses of grey limestone. A few feet of Purbeck beds consisting of limestone and marl with fossils outcrop in some places at Shotover, but

Fig. 3 Geological map of Shotover

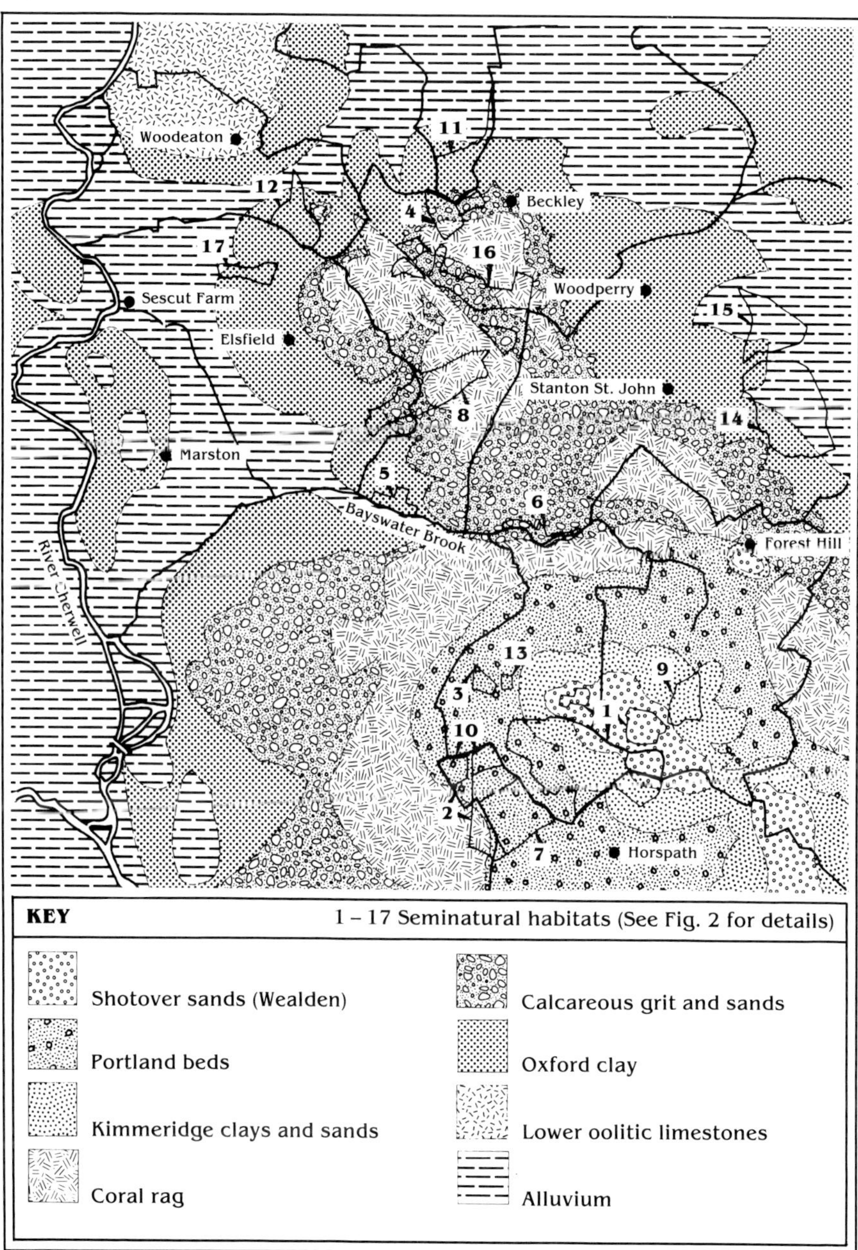

KEY   1 – 17 Seminatural habitats (See Fig. 2 for details)

Shotover sands (Wealden)

Portland beds

Kimmeridge clays and sands

Coral rag

Calcareous grit and sands

Oxford clay

Lower oolitic limestones

Alluvium

their occurrence is sporadic.

The top 15 metres or so of Shotover Hill is composed of clays and sands of Wealden age. They contain some freshwater fossils which were probably deposited in an enormous estuary which covered much of southern Britain at this time. The gravelly residue of weathered ironsand has produced a steep-sided hill. These ironsands are known as Shotover Sands and consist of ferruginous and argillaceous loams, ochre, yellow sand and ferruginous soil with many fragments of ironsand. A number of freshwater fossils have been discovered and it is possible that at least some of the beds were deposited in a large, freshwater lake. Indeed, dinosaur footprints have been discovered in Shotover Sands where they outcrop in Wiltshire.

Alongside the river Cherwell are very recent deposits of river borne material called alluvium. This alluvium is thousands rather than millions of years old and bones found in alluvium near Oxford show that local fauna included mammoth, woolly rhinoceros, bison and cave lion.

Shotover's streams drain to the river Cherwell via either the Bayswater brook or river Ray. There are many springs on both Shotover and Forest hills, which arise at the junction of permeable and impermeable rocks. The spring-fed streams are small and only hold any quantity of water after heavy rain.

To sum up the flatter land surrounding Shotover Hill consists of alluvium, clays and limestones, whereas the hill itself and the outlying Forest Hill consists of thin bands of limestones, clays and sandstones with the latter predominating.

Chapter 4

Grassland

A variety of different types of grassland are found at Shotover. Many fields have been 'improved' by treating with fertilizers or by being ploughed and resown. Such fields are dominated by a small number of cultivars of productive grasses and are of limited value to wildlife. However, some grasslands remain which are less intensively managed and may be described as seminatural. It must be remembered that if it were not for the effects of man and his grazing animals these fields would rapidly revert to scrub and woodland. An aerial photograph shows that the Horseshoe field on the south side of Shotover Hill was ploughed in 1947[23], but by the 1980s thick scrub had developed with oaks up to 8 metres in height.

Shotover's grasslands may be classified according to the soils on which they occur. The acidic soils on the slopes of Shotover Hill support a fine-leaved, hill-pasture type sward. A few small remnants of limestone grassland are found where Coral Rag outcrops. In addition where the soil is deeper and the pH close to 7, neutral grasslands occur.

Acid grassland

Acid grassland is found where the soil is well drained on the higher slopes of Shotover Hill. In former times the grassland was maintained by grazing – cattle, sheep, horses, deer and rabbits would have all played a part in preventing much woody regrowth. Nowadays organized grazing has ceased except for some small areas on the northern slopes, and it is the trample of human feet and the grazing of rabbits which maintain the grassland as such.

Acid grassland supports a smaller number of flowering plants than limestone grassland. However, many attractive plants can be found. In addition to the dominant bent grasses (*Agrostis canina* and *A. capillaris*), heath bedstraw (*Galium saxatile*), trailing St. John's-wort (*Hypericum humifusum*), squirreltail fescue (*Vulpia bromoides*), early hair-grass (*Aira praecox*), knotted trefoil (*Trifolium striatum*), heath speedwell (*Veronica officinalis*), bird's-foot (*Ornithopus perpusillus*), sand spurrey (*Spergularia rubra*) and common centaury (*Centaurium erythraea*) are still found. There are common mosses such as *Dicranum scoparium*, *Ceratodon purpureus* and *Pottia truncata* as well as more local species such as *Campylopus pyriformis*, *Brachythecium albicans* and *Polytrichum juniperinum*.

Many interesting plants are known to have been lost from this habitat. Subterranean trefoil (*Trifolium subterraneum*), broad-leaved cudweed (*Filago pyramidata*), small-flowered buttercup (*Ranunculus parviflorus*), small-flowered catchfly (*Silene gallica*), bur chervil (*Anthriscus caucaulis*), mat-grass (*Nardus stricta*), buck's-horn plantain (*Plantago coronopus*),

autumn lady's-tresses (*Spiranthes spiralis*), and field gentian (*Gentianella campestris*) are documented examples of extinctions. Bryophytes lost include *Pogonatum nanum*, *P. aloides*, and *Climacium dendroides*.

The woodlark is a bird which nested at Shotover until the 1950s and has a requirement for short-grazed turf and bare ground. The loss of this uncommon bird may have followed the rapid scrub encroachment which was a result of the decimation of the rabbit population by myxomatosis in 1954. In the 1980s Shotover's rabbit population, although still prone to great fluctuations, seems to be maintaining itself at a high level. Some of the areas of scrub on the south side of Shotover Hill have been removed as a conservation measure. It will be interesting to see whether any of the lost plants return.

Neutral grassland

At the base of Shotover Hill on the lower Kimmeridge beds and the Coral Rag, are some interesting fields best described as neutral grassland. These fields are related to the nearby Yarnton and Pixey Meads which are extraordinarily rich in wild flowers. Unfortunately the Shotover grasslands do not have the richness of top quality meadows, but a good deal of interest still remains. On the south side of Shotover Hill are the two Slade Camp fields and 'Haynes' field, a few small meadows remain near Lower Farm alongside the Bayswater Brook to the west of Shotover Hill and to the north-west of the hill is Beckley Common.

One of the Bayswater meadows with the buildings of Lower Farm

Grassland

Lower Farm meadows Alongside the Bayswater Brook, just to the north of Barton Estate and close to Lower Farm, are some attractive small meadows about 15 ha in extent. The meadows are cattle grazed and their present ecological health is the result of sympathetic management by the local farmer. It is likely that if ever the farm changed hands the fields would be threatened by agricultural improvement. Indeed, one of the fields was sold in 1981 and it was immediately ploughed resulting in the loss of a colony of green-winged orchids (*Orchis morio*).

The soil is wet for much of the year but supports a rich flora including greater burnet (*Sanguisorba officinalis*), yellow rattle (*Rhinanthus minor*), ragged-robin (*Lychnis flos-cuculi*), burnet-saxifrage (*Pimpinella saxifraga*) and sneezewort (*Achillea ptarmica*) with brooklime (*Veronica beccabunga*) and marsh-marigold (*Caltha palustris*) in the wettest areas.

Slade Camp fields The two Slade Camp fields have a similar appearance with areas of grassland being interspersed with trees and patches of scrub. The southerly field is part of the only field which belonged to Brasenose Farm until its sale to Oxford Corporation in 1935. The westerly part of this field was taken for the construction of the Slade Isolation Hospital in the late 1930s, and the present boundaries were determined by the construction of a dual carriageway road (the Eastern Bypass) in the early 1960s. The northerly Slade Camp field includes one and a half of the fields (Elder Stubs Ground and part of Middle Ground) which were formerly part of Wood Farm. Middle Ground, as well as Magdalen Wood, was bisected by the construction of the Eastern Bypass.

Slade Camp south with Brasenose Wood in the background

Grassland

Both Slade Camp fields were used for army dwellings during and after the
Second World War. Although Oxford was not bombed during the war it is
interesting that the Slade Camp fields were clearly marked as bomb
targets on 1940 Luftwaffe maps[24]. The military buildings were used for
temporary housing by the local authority until their demolition in the late
1960s. Many garden trees and shrubs, such as laburnum and sumach, are
found in these fields. At present (1983) the northerly field is used only for
informal recreation, but the southerly field is let to a farmer who cuts an
annual hay crop and winter grazes cattle.

A wide range of grasses occur in these two fields including perennial rye-
grass (*Lolium perenne*), false oat-grass (*Arrhenatherum elatius*), rough
meadow-grass (*Poa trivialis*), crested dog's-tail (*Cynosurus cristatus*), soft-
brome (*Bromus hordeaceus*) and creeping bent (*Agrostis stolonifera*). Many
legumes are present including common bird's-foot trefoil (*Lotus corniculatus*), white clover (*Trifolium repens*), red clover (*T. pratense*), hop trefoil
(*T. campestre*), grass vetchling (*Lathyrus nissolia*), meadow vetchling (*L.
pratensis*) and the rare tuberous pea (*L. tuberosus*). The presence of alsike
clover (*Trifolium hybridum*) in the southerly Slade Camp field is an indication of its former use for clover cultivation[25]. Other interesting plants
include the parasitic common broomrape (*Orobanche minor*), goat's rue
(*Galega officinalis*), creeping bellflower (*Campanula rapunculoides*) and
woolly thistle (*Cirsium eriophorum*).

These fields are valuable for birds. Notably skylark and grasshopper
warbler bred in some years between 1975 – 83 and tree pipits display
regularly although nesting has not been confirmed. Stonechats and wheatears are occasionally seen on winter passage migration. Lepidoptera are
abundant here. Marbled whites and common blues are two of the many
butterflies which breed in these fields. The 5-spot burnet moth provides a
most spectacular sight here. A 'mark and recapture' estimate of the
numbers of this red and black moth in 1979 suggested that there were
50,000 in the northerly Slade Camp field. Other interesting day-flying
moths are the latticed heath (*Semiothisa clathrata*), mother shipton
(*Callistega mi*) and the burnet companion (*Euclidia glyphica*).

Haynes field A gently sloping grassland, Haynes field leads up to
a reservoir near the top of Shotover Hill. This meadow is sporadically
grazed by cattle and horses and occasionally cut for hay. The flowery
upper slopes of the field are clearly visible from the Oxford Bypass, the
construction of which reduced the area of this field.

Grasses present include meadow oat-grass (*Avenula pratensis*), meadow
foxtail (*Alopecurus pratensis*) and perennial rye-grass (*Lolium perenne*).
This is one of the most colourful of the Shotover neutral grasslands in
summer, with plants such as greater burnet (*Sanguisorba officinalis*),
common spotted-orchid (*Dactylorhiza fuchsii*), burnet-saxifrage (*Pimpinella saxifraga*), common fleabane (*Pulicaria dysenterica*) and devil's-bit
scabious (*Succisa pratensis*).

Butterflies and moths abound here with marbled whites and 5-spot burnets being abundant in some years. Stonechats are regularly seen in this field on winter passage migration.

Beckley Common Sloping down from the Beckley – Elsfield road towards Noke Wood, much of Beckley Common has been improved, but there are several wet areas with interesting plants. As its name suggests the meadow was formerly common grazing for the parish of Beckley, and the Common is shown as much more extensive on a seventeenth century map[12]. Nowadays the Common is in private hands but it is still subject to cattle grazing.

The grassland has few plants of interest with common grasses such as perennial rye-grass (*Lolium perenne*), meadow foxtail (*Alopecurus pratensis*) and smooth meadow-grass (*Poa pratensis*). The wet areas have a more interesting flora including giant horsetail (*Equisetum telmateia*), lesser spearwort (*Ranunculus flammula*), common fleabane (*Pulicaria dysenterica*), wood small-reed (*Calamagrostis epigejos*) and common spotted-orchid (*Dactylorhiza fuchsii*).

Limestone grassland

Where the Coral Rag is exposed and the soils are thin, a rich calcicolous flora occurs where the land has not been 'improved' or converted to arable. These calcareous soils are fertile and consequently almost all are used for intensive agriculture. The largest remnants are within the Sydling's Copse nature reserve owned by the Berkshire, Buckinghamshire and Oxfordshire Naturalists' Trust (BBONT), and the only other small remnants are on steeply sloping land close to the Bayswater Brook.

Limestone grassland is very rich in wild flowers. A total of 127 species of flowering plant have been recorded from the 1.5 ha field alongside Sydling's Copse. Upright brome (*Bromus erectus*) is the dominant grass and many other attractive plants are to be seen including common rock-rose (*Helianthemum nummularium*), wild liquorice (*Astragalus glycyphyllos*), cowslip (*Primula veris*), viper's-bugloss (*Echium vulgare*), common eye-bright (*Euphrasia nemorosa*), thyme (*Thymus pulegioides* and *T. praecox*), wild basil (*Clinopodium vulgare*), ploughman's-spikenard (*Inula conyza*) and carline thistle (*Carlina vulgaris*). In addition several shrubs and sapling trees have become established including wayfaring-tree (*Viburnum lantana*), guelder-rose (*V. opulus*), wild privet (*Ligustrum vulgare*) and dog rose (*Rosa canina*).

In late spring and early summer this grassland is a splendid sight with many colourful flowers and abundant insect life. 29 species of butterfly have been seen here including strong colonies of marbled white and dark green fritillary, as well as such species as green hairstreak, white-letter hairstreak (last seen 1981) and brown argus. In former times this grassland was probably used as a racehorse gallop[12] but in recent years BBONT has introduced a grazing and cutting regime to maintain the floral diversity.

A second smaller area of limestone grassland occurs within the BBONT nature reserve which supports a slightly different flora including woolly thistle (*Cirsium eriophorum*) and bee orchid (*Ophrys apifera*). Other minute remnants of limestone grassland are to be found on the slopes above the Bayswater Brook. To the north of the brook is a small flowery corner, less than 0.5 ha in extent, which has more than 80 flowering plants including clustered bellflower (*Campanula glomerata*), horseshoe vetch (*Hippocrepis comosa*), common rock-rose (*Helianthemum nummularium*), dropwort (*Filipendula vulgaris*) and quaking-grass (*Briza media*). A nearby roadside verge, now a county council picnic site, has a rich flora including kidney vetch (*Anthyllis vulneraria*), blue fleabane (*Erigeron acer*), common corn-salad (*Valerianella locusta*) and vervain (*Verbena officinalis*). To the south of the Bayswater Brook is a small area of limestone grassland in Sandhills.

Limestone grassland within Sydling's Copse nature reserve

Grassland

This grassland is lightly scrubbed over but supports plants such as fairy flax (*Linum catharticum*), wild thyme (*Thymus drucei*) and quaking-grass (*Briza media*).

The Sydling's Copse and Bayswater Brook area was as well known to early botanists as was Shotover Hill. Indeed George Claridge Druce writes in the second edition of his Flora of Oxfordshire[27]

> 'Stow Wood and Headington Wick form perhaps the most interesting portion of botanizing country in Central England, the riches of which were known to Gerard, William Cole, Ashmole and the early samplers. Situated on the Corallian beds the upper portion of which has weathered into dry, friable sand, through which here and there streams have cut their way down to the underlying clay, they afford suitable habitats for a most varied flora'.

Several calcicoles have been lost from this area including autumn gentian (*Gentianella amarella*), hairy rock-cress (*Arabis hirsuta*), shining

A fragment of limestone grassland surrounded by arable fields alongside Bayswater Brook

cranes bill (*Geranium lucidum*) and squinancy wort (*Asperula cyanchica*).
Although it is not possible to locate precisely where these plants grew, it
seems probable that some of them were found on the meadow to the north
of Bayswater Brook.

Chapter 5

Heathland

Heathland is characteristically dominated by heather (*Calluna vulgaris*) and is usually found on well drained, acidic soils. Such soils are rare in the Oxford area and consequently heath is an uncommon habitat. The nearest region of extensive heathland is found on the tertiary gravel beds of south and east Berkshire. The largest expanse of heathland is found on the south side of Shotover Hill where Shotover Sands outcrop. A much smaller remnant is found to the north of Sydling's Copse.

To set the scene Druce in the first decade of the twentieth century writes[3]

> *'The once celebrated district of Shotover has suffered much during the past century, at the beginning of which it was to a great extent open and uncultivated ground, in parts thickly wooded and in others showing delightful expanses of heath. In some places where the water issued at the base of previous strata bogs were formed, then the home of sundew, wood horsetail and other interesting uliginal species, while the drier spots on the sandy or peaty soils had the buck's-horn plantain and two species of clubmoss; in other spots the moss Polytrichum commune was luxuriant, while on the turfy slopes the moonwort, the lady's tresses and the field gentian delighted the wanderer, or on the heathy ground the mountain fern showed its fragrant fronds. But these have gone. The inclosure of the heathy slopes, the cultivation of its surface, the various encroachments upon its domain, have gradually denuded the hill of its characteristic vegetation and the progress of destruction still goes on. Year by year there is a shrinkage of the original vegetation and an extension of the plants which follow in the wake of man's disturbance of nature's domain. There are, however, still to be found some species of considerable interest . . .'*

Many heathland plants have become extinct at Shotover. Stag's horn clubmoss (*Lycopodium clavatum*), fir clubmoss (*Huperzia selago*), mountain fern (*Thelypteris limbosperma*), buck's-horn plantain (*Plantago coronopus*), wood sage (*Teucrium scorodonia*), small cudweed (*Logfia minima*), bristle club-rush (*Scirpus setaceus*), sheep's-bit (*Jasione montana*), bur chervil (*Anthriscus caucaulis*) and rat's-tail fescue (*Vulpia myuros*) have all been lost from Shotover.

Some of the oldest bryophyte collections in the world are from Shotover and known heathland extinctions include *Nardia scalaris, Solenostoma crenulatum, Tetraphis pellucida, Polytrichum piliferum* and *Racomitrium canescens*[28,29].

Of the insects the green tiger beetle *Cicindela campestris*, the ground beetle *Carabus gallicus* and the nationally rare oil beetle *Meloe rugosus* are all thought to be extinct[3]. Several heath-nesting bird species have been lost, notably the red-backed shrike (now a national rarity), nightjar, wheatear, stonechat and whinchat.

All in all we are presented with a picture of dramatic decline in both quantity and quality of the heathland habitat. Heather's presence is determined by a complex of factors. Moist air and free drainage are necessary to heather, as is a highly acid soil which permits the existence of the symbiotic fungus *Phoma* on which heather depends in nature. For dominance of heath some factor which prevents gregarious and successful establishment of trees is essential, be it fires, high intensity grazing or violent winds. Heaths of southern Britain are normally associated with sandy or gravelly soils and typically contain very few species of higher plants apart from heather, although there are usually several species of bryophyte and lichen present.

There is some heather remaining at Shotover but rarely in sufficient quantities to constitute a true heath. Large quantities of silver birch, gorse and bracken remain which are species often associated with heaths, but with the cessation of grazing and burning the remaining heathland plants are becoming less numerous.

Small quantities of pill sedge (*Carex pilulifera*), tormentil (*Potentilla erecta*), slender trefoil (*Trifolium micranthum*) and knotted trefoil (*T. striatum*) may be found as well as typical heathland bryophytes such as *Pleurozium schreberi* and *Campylopus pyriformis* and lichens including *Cladonia allosquamosa, C. chlorophaea, C. fimbiata, C. pyxidata* and *C. subulata.*

The small remnant of heath to the north of Sydling's Copse is no more than 1 ha in extent, and as with the remaining heath on Shotover Hill has a dense covering of bracken. However, the small area of high quality heathland habitat has several local species including early forget-me-not (*Myosotis ramosissima*) which produces its miniature inflorescences in April, lesser chickweed (*Stellaria pallida*), early hair-grass (*Aira praecox*) and silver hair-grass (*A. caryophyllea*) as well as a little heather.

Heathland has declined dramatically both in area and richness in lowland England. The loss of the Dorset heaths is well documented and they are now only 15% of their 1760 extent[30]. The reason for the decline in heathland throughout lowland England is that heaths can be readily converted for agriculture. Improved mechanisation and availability of fertilisers allow heaths to be ploughed and turned to arable usage. However, because of the intrinsic low fertility of heathland soil, crop production is often poor. As at Shotover some of the former heathland may be uneconomic to farm and so allowed to revert to its former status. There is no doubt that with management to prevent encroachment of woody species and to decrease the dominance of bracken, Shotover's heathland will regain some of its former interest and attractiveness.

Chapter 6

Wetlands

Wetlands are one of the most threatened wildlife habitats in lowland Britain. Until the beginning of the nineteenth century large areas of East Anglia were marsh and fen. More locally Otmoor was a substantial area of wet moorland until the Inclosure Acts of the mid-nineteenth century. With an improved understanding of drainage technology these wetlands have been relentlessly drained and turned into high quality agricultural land. Marsh, fen and bog occurred in some quantity within Shotover Royal Forest. Following disafforestation in 1660 the wetlands were drained and converted to agriculture with the subsequent loss of many plant and animal species.

There are three categories of wetland remaining at Shotover: marsh, fen and pond. Marsh is a wet area where the water is close to, but not above ground level, and where the soil pH is acidic. Fen is a corresponding habitat on alkaline soils where there is some accumulation of surface peat. Shotover's numerous ponds are all artificial and of relatively recent origin.

Marsh

The number and extent of marshes on the slopes of Shotover have declined dramatically over the past 200 years. This loss is testified to by a catalogue of extinctions. Round-leaved sundew (*Drosera rotundifolia*), wood horsetail (*Equisetum sylvaticum*), flat-sedge (*Blysmus compressus*), bog pimpernel (*Anagallis tenella*), blinks (*Montia fontana*) and crested buckler-fern (*Dryopteris cristata*) have all been lost. Of the bryophytes, *Polytrichum commune* is known to have been destroyed by drainage

'Polytrichum commune was formerly fine at Shotover but destroyed by drainage about 1861' [26]

Other examples of peat bog bryophytes which once grew at Shotover include *Cephalozia connivens, Lepidozia setacea, Sphagnum subnitens, S. squarrosum, S. palustre, Dicranella cerviculata, Dicranum bonjeanii, Splachnum ampullaceum, Philonotis fontana* and *Drepanocladus revolvens*[28,29].

The reason for the dramatic decline in wetland species is that the former marshes were drained and converted to agricultural use. A few small marshes still exist alongside the spring-fed streams which drain Johnson's Piece and Holme Ground. Plants such as the spectacular marsh-marigold with its large, bright yellow, buttercup-like flowers can still be found, as well as opposite-leaved golden saxifrage (*Chrysosplenium oppositifolium*), marsh valerian (*Valeriana dioica*), marsh stichwort (*Stellaria alsine*), hard

Marsh within Johnson's Piece on the south side of Shotover Hill

rush (*Juncus inflexus*), soft rush (*J. effusus*), jointed rush (*J. articulatus*) and small quantities of the local flea sedge (*Carex pulicaris*). Several locally scarce species of bryophyte such as *Pellia epiphylla*, *Cephalozia bicuspidata*, *Calypogeia fissa* and *Rhizomnium punctatum* can still be found. But these small marshes are being further diminished by invasion of sallow scrub and willow herb.

Fen

A small fen community exists alongside the stream which bisects Sydling's and Wick Copse. This type of fen community is rare in England but an out-standing example is found at Cothill near Abingdon. Plants still to be found at Sydling's Copse include fragrant orchid (*Gymnadenia conopsea*) with its carnation-like smell, bog pimpernel (*Anagallis tenella*), fen bed-straw (*Galium uliginosum*), hemp-agrimony (*Eupatorium cannabinum*), brookweed (*Samolus valerandi*), marsh helleborine (*Epipactis palustris*), blunt-flowered rush (*Juncus subnodulosus*), flea sedge (*Carex pulicaris*), long-stalked yellow-sedge (*C. lepidocarpa*) and black bog-rush (*Schoenus nigricans*). In addition columbine (*Aquilegia vulgaris*) grows on tussocks in the fen, although this plant is usually said to favour woodlands. A rich assemblage of bryophytes grow between the tussocks, including *Drepano-cladus uncinatus*.

The main threat to this community is natural succession, with woody plants such as grey willow and aspen shading and drying out the fen plants. One species known to have been lost from this fen is Grass-of-Parnassus (*Parnassia palustris*).

Birds of interest which breed here include sedge warbler, grasshopper warbler and reed bunting. The stream itself is inhabited by the local fresh-water crayfish.

Ponds

There are several ponds and small lakes at Shotover. At the foot of the north-west slopes of the hill are three ponds, each about 0.5 ha in extent, and several smaller ponds. These are the result of excavations for bricking clay in the nineteenth and early twentieth centuries. A cascade of four ponds occur in Shotover Spinney on the northern slopes of Shotover Hill. These brick-dammed ponds were probably constructed as a trout hatchery. A large, rectangular pond forms part of the landscaped gardens of Shotover House laid out in the eighteenth century.

Water plants associated with these ponds include water-crowfoot (*Ranunculus aquatilis*), bulrush (*Typha latifolia*) and Canadian pondweed (*Elodea canadensis*). The uncommon grass-wrack pondweed (*Potomogeton compressus*) has been recorded from Shotover Spinney.

Of the invertebrates a noticeable feature is the number of freshwater

Valley fen in gulley of stream which drains Sydling's Copse and College Pond

mussels (*Unionidae*) in the large rectangular pond near Shotover House. All ponds have many common invertebrates such as water boatmen, pond skaters and water beetles. Several species of dragonfly and damselfly breed in these ponds. Examples include *Aeshna juncea, A. grandis,* the migrant *A. mixta, Sympetrum striolatum* and the two common damselflies *Coenagrion puella* and *Ischnura elegans.*

Toads and frogs breed in these ponds in large numbers. In March and April the ponds ring with the amphibian mating calls, and the resulting masses of frogspawn and strips of toadspawn are readily seen. All three British newts have been recorded including the uncommon crested newt.

Several interesting species of bird breed on and near the ponds, including coot, moorhen, dabchick and mallard. Reed warblers inhabit the reed beds near the largest pond. Other birds regularly seen include grey wagtail and kingfisher, but nesting has not been confirmed.

In most ways the wildlife habitats of Shotover have declined in quantity and quality since royal forest times, but this does not apply to open waters. There would have been few ponds in Shotover Royal Forest. However, a lake called *Wodetonehoo* situated near Woodeaton, is mentioned in the 1298 perambulation, and the Domesday entry for Headington mentions

'five fisheries for Headington'[1]

In Sydling's Copse there is a man-made earth-dam, probably medieval in origin, which suggests that there may have been a 'pot pond' to rear fish for the kitchen. However, there are certainly more ponds now and consequently plants and animals which depend on this freshwater habitat have been encouraged.

Old clay-pit pond within BBONT Henry Stephen / C.S. Lewis reserve

Chapter 7

Scrub and Hedges

Scrub

Scrub is the name given to a community of plants dominated by shrubs or bushes. At Shotover scrub occurs where heathland or grassland has ceased to be managed and invasion by woody plants has occurred. Scrub is a transitional habitat in that if left undisturbed it will develop into woodland.

On the higher slopes of the hill many hectares of scrub developed on fields which were formerly used for agriculture. Mary Sadler's field, Sand pit field and Horseshoe field all have substantial stands of scrub. The last mentioned field may be seen to have been ploughed in 1947 from an available aerial photograph[23]. The scrub is dominated by hawthorn and pedunculate oak with lesser quantities of blackthorn, elder, sycamore, ash and rowan. An interesting feature of this scrub is the presence of a single wild service tree (*Sorbus torminalis*) sapling. Very few herbaceous plants are able to tolerate the deep shade under this scrub, but there are some shade-tolerant species such as ground-ivy (*Glechoma hederacea*) and cuckoo pint (*Arum maculatum*), as well as the abundant moss *Eurhynchium praelongum*.

A slightly different scrub community has developed on the periphery of Brasenose Wood, particularly in Open Brasenose and Slade Camp north. Here the community is dominated by blackthorn with lesser quantities of buckthorn, hawthorn, elder, crab apple and pedunculate oak. A special feature of this area of scrub is the presence of a nationally rare butterfly – the black hairstreak, which may be seen flitting amongst the upper branches of the blackthorn bushes at the end of June and the beginning of July.

Where scrub has developed on limestone soils, such as the steep slopes of the Bayswater Brook valley, additional shrubs present include wild privet, wayfaring-tree, guelder-rose and spindle.

A different scrub community has developed on the wet, calcareous soils of the stream which drains Sydling's Copse and College Pond. Here the fen tends to be invaded by ash, grey willow and aspen. In many ways this area is reminiscent of carr but the absence of alder precludes the use of the term. The growth of this type of scrub considerably reduces the floral diversity of the area but provides habitat for a different range of insects.

Although the plant diversity of scrub is poor it is a valuable habitat for many birds. Magpie, jay, wren, blackbird, thrush, chaffinch, whitethroat, lesser whitethroat, willow warbler, blackcap and garden warbler all commonly nest in Shotover's scrub. In addition, nightingales breed sporadically in this habitat although they are now much more rarely heard than in the years before the Second World War. Scrub also provides a

Hawthorn scrub on southern slopes of Shotover – note the total lack of ground flora

valuable winter food supply for many birds – fieldfares and redwings are regularly seen feeding on hips and haws in frosty weather.

Hedges

Hedges are known to be particularly valuable to many forms of wildlife. Several species of bird nest in hedges and others feed on hedgerow fruits in autumn and winter. Small rodents find shelter in the longer vegetation at the base of hedges. Hedges are important to many species of insect which tend to fly alongside hedges rather than across inhospitable land. Indeed hedges are especially important refuges for wildlife in intensively-farmed arable areas. There are many hedgerows at Shotover but the majority are of recent origin. Such hedges, with only one or two shrub species, are of limited value to wildlife. Ancient hedges, which may possess up to 15 different shrubs, are much more valuable to wildlife and have a wide range of associated plants, mammals and invertebrates.

There are very few ancient hedgerows within the boundary of Shotover Royal Forest. However, the hedges on the north and south boundaries of Shotover Plain contain hawthorn, blackthorn, wild plum, oak, ash, holly, elder, hazel and gorse in addition to the introduced Scots pine and larch. The hedgerows have about 6.5 woody species per 30 yards and this dates them at about 700 years old according to the method of Hooper[32]. This method depends on hedges acquiring a single additional woody species each century by natural colonization.

Chapter 8

Woodland

Shotover's woodland has suffered much less than the other seminatural habitats and about 241 ha of relatively unspoilt woodland remain. These woods are shown on the first edition O.S. maps and hence may be termed ancient woodlands. Indeed most of the woods are mentioned by name in the 1298 perambulation[7], and it is likely that they have been wooded since the colonization by woodland following the last ice age.

Although the woodlands are found on a variety of different soils, the range of trees and shrubs within the woods is remarkably uniform. Pedunculate oak is always the dominant tree. Wild cherry and field maple occur as trees in all of Shotover's woods and indeed the presence of some splendid old cherries is a striking feature of the Shotover woods. Aspen grows abundantly in the wetter parts of several of the woods. Although individual trees rarely attain great size or age the success of vegetative propagation from root suckers leads to very dense stands. In parts of Brasenose Wood coppice clearance is followed by rapid growth (up to 2m per year) of aspen shoots. Such rapid growth, coupled with their apparent unpalatability to browsing deer, soon leads to thick stands of young aspen trees. Silver birch is found in all of the woods. It is most abundant on the lighter, sandy soils but it tolerates all the soil conditions. However, the hot dry summers of 1975 and 1976 caused a high mortality amongst birches on clay soils. The closely related downy birch is widely but thinly spread at Shotover. Ash occurs in most of the woods but is more frequent as coppice growth than as a timber tree. It may be that past management favoured the use of ash as underwood rather than for its timber, or that, as in the New Forest, centuries of browsing prevented its establishment. Rowan occurs in many Shotover woods but never attains great size.

Trees which occur in lesser numbers include English elm, the adults of which have all perished from Dutch Elm disease. Invasive, suckering elm clones still occur in several of the woods. Wych elm formerly occurred in some of the woods but is now gone from most and only remains as low growth in others. A scattering of the evergreen yew and holly are to be found in the southerly woods – the latter only growing to tree proportions on the higher, lighter soils. Wild service tree occurs sparingly in the eastern woods, probably as a result of spreading from Bernwood Forest. Several of the woods have stands of beech which include some mature trees. However, it is probable that these trees result from recent plantings and it is unlikely that beech is indigenous at Shotover. Sycamore occurs in most of the woods but is not plentiful.

A wide range of shrubs is present – a feature typical of lowland ancient woodlands. The commonest species are hazel, hawthorn, Midland hawthorn, dogwood and blackthorn. In lesser numbers are holly, gorse, crab apple, elder, goat willow, grey willow, wild privet, guelder-rose, wayfaring-tree, spindle and buckthorn – the last three mentioned species being virtually confined to woods on calcareous soils.

The shrub or coppice layer is still actively worked in Brasenose and Holly woods. The shrubs are cut to ground level on a rotational basis every 10 years or so. In former times the cut wood was of great value for fuel, building, fences and for various country crafts. There is a record in the 1933 Forest Hill Year Book[33] of a family named Soanes who made sheep hurdles and oak laths for roofing from local underwood. The Soanes family is said to have followed this trade since at least the early nineteenth century.

An exceptional range of herbaceous species grow in the Shotover woods. This diversity is another striking feature of ancient woodlands in lowland Britain. In Brasenose Wood for example, nearly 200 herbaceous species have been recorded over the period 1975 – 82. One reason for this diversity is that the traditional coppicing management has been maintained for many centuries. Among the more interesting of Shotover's herbaceous species are columbine (*Aquilegia vulgaris*), greater burnet-saxifrage (*Pimpinella major*), water avens (*Geum rivale*), toothwort (*Lathraea squamaria*), herb-Paris (*Paris quadrifolia*), wild daffodil (*Narcissus pseudonarcissus*), meadow saffron (*Colchicum autumnale*), violet helleborine (*Epipactis purpurata*) and green-flowered helleborine (*E. phyllanthes*), although no single wood contains all of these species.

Although Shotover's woodland has suffered less than the other habitats some extinctions have occurred since Druce's time, including tutsan (*Hypericum androseanum*), bitter vetch (*Lathyrus montanus*) and greater bellflower (*Campanula latifolia*).

A number of epiphytic bryophytes which grow on tree bark, have been lost from Shotover. Species lost include *Radula complanata, Orthotrichum striatum, Ulota phyllantha, Cryphaea heteromalla, Leucodon sciuroides* and *Neckera complanata*[28,29]. Shotover's remaining epiphyte flora is disappointingly species-poor. In part this is due to Oxford's low rainfall compared to the woods of western Britain, which are exceptionally rich in bryophytes and lichens, and in part due to atmospheric pollution from the nearby industrial complex. Further evidence for this latter suggestion comes from a detailed study of epiphytic lichens which are sensitive indicators of atmospheric pollution (see Appendix 3).

A more detailed look at each of Shotover's remaining seminatural woods follows.

Brasenose Wood

The most southerly of Shotover's woods, lying on Kimmeridge clay at the base of Shotover Hill, Brasenose Wood contains many mature trees which give the wood a splendid and distinctive atmosphere. An active coppicing policy has given the wood the whole range of underwood age-classes. The extensive system of rides, provided because the wood is a public amenity, results in many flowery margins which are both attractive and of high

nature conservation value.

Post Royal Forest history   There were a number of disputes in the sixteenth and seventeenth centuries over grazing rights of commoners within Brasenose Wood. For example in 1570 there was a dispute concerning whether

'oxen, sheepe, or labouring horse can common within the forest'[43]

In 1789 Open Brasenose was used for common grazing by the parishes of Headington, Horspath and Cowley, and so it seems that the disputes about grazing in Brasenose Wood were resolved by allowing common grazing rights in the 26.74 acres of Open Brasenose. In the nineteenth and early twentieth centuries gypsies camped in Open Brasenose, but this practice ceased and the common was fenced following an incident where a gypsy man stabbed his wife to death there, and was later hanged[44].

10 acres of woodland were felled in 1852 – 3 and converted to arable usage[41]. Judging from the 1797 map of Richard Davis[42] the parcel of woodland was removed from the north-west of the woods. By the early years of the twentieth century Brasenose Farm was becoming uneconomic; demand for timber and coppice wood was slack and the shallow-soiled single field was unproductive. Church[49] states that Brasenose Wood's underwood was in poor condition in 1921 – 22 when it fetched only £4 per acre (= 6d per pole) at the annual underwood sales, compared to £6 per acre for the better quality underwood of Bagley Wood and £14 per acre for best quality coppice in Nuneham Wood. Coppicing has long since ceased in Bagley Wood, to be replaced by conifer production.

In 1935 Brasenose College sold Brasenose Wood to the Citizens of Oxford for £6,000 on condition that

'The piece of land marked Brasenose Wood . . . shall for ever be kept and used as woodland and no timber be felled . . . unless it is in the interests of good forestry'.[45]

Wildlife   Brasenose Wood contains virtually all of the trees and shrubs found in the rest of the Shotover woods – for an 18.5 ha woodland it is exceptionally diverse. The field layer contains no real rarities and indeed only a few species that are even locally uncommon. However, the variety and colour of spring flowers is a wonderful sight.

In late March and April wood anemones (*Anemone nemorosa*), lesser celandines (*Ranunculus ficaria*) and bluebells (*Hyacinthoides non-scripta*) grow in profusion. Slightly later appear greater stichwort (*Stellaria holostea*), bugle (*Ajuga reptans*) and yellow archangel (*Lamiastrum galeobdolon*). In June and July common spotted-orchid (*Dactylorhiza fuchsii*), saw-wort (*Serratula tinctoria*) and betony (*Stachys officinalis*) provide an impressive display of colour. It is in the summer that some of the more unusual plants such as violet helleborine (*Epipactis purpurata*), greater burnet-saxifrage (*Pimpinella major*) and orpine (*Sedum telephium*) may be seen in flower.

Woodland

Several species of fern grow in the woods including bracken (*Pteridium aquilinium*), male fern (*Dryopteris filix-mas*), scaly male fern (*D. borreri*), broad buckler-fern (*D. dilatata*) and narrow buckler-fern (*D. carthusiana*). Under the field layer are many bryophytes including *Mnium hornum, Thuidium tamariscinum, Atrichum undulatum* and *Eurhynchium praelongum. Funaria hygrometrica* and *Bryum pallens* may be seen on fire-scars and *Pleuridium acuminatum* grows on rabbit scrapes. The uncommon *Dicranum tauricum* grows as an epiphyte on the branches of oak trees.

Such a floristically rich wood is likely to support a rich fauna and indeed this is the case. The most readily seen mammals are grey squirrel, rabbit, fox and muntjac. Also present are hedgehog, weasel, common shrew, pygmy shrew, water shrew, pipistrelle bat, bank vole, field vole, wood mouse, harvest mouse and house mouse, which are all resident breeders. Stoat, badger and fallow deer have all been seen on occasions but are probably not resident.

A detailed survey over the period 1978 – 83 showed that in Brasenose Wood proper (excluding Open Brasenose) about 225 pairs of birds nest each year. 34 regular breeding species include sparrow-hawk, stock dove, cuckoo, tawny owl, green and greater spotted woodpeckers, mistle thrush, marsh tit, willow tit, jay and bullfinch. Occasional breeders include pied wagtail, kestrel and whitethroat, and species which are regularly seen but not thought to breed include lesser spotted woodpecker, wood warbler and redpoll.

No rare species of bird occur in Brasenose Wood but the variety and number of breeding birds is impressive. The volume of bird song in April and May is striking and it is sufficient to almost blot out the road noise from the nearby Oxford Bypass. It is interesting to note that there are almost 12 nests per hectare in the woodland – a several times greater density of nests than in the surrounding farmland.

The insect life of Brasenose Wood is very rich. 23 species of butterfly have been recorded including the nationally rare black hairstreak. Other butterflies of note include purple hairstreak and white admiral. Over 200 species of moth have been recorded including sprawler (*Brachionycha sphinx*), scarce silver lines (*Pseudoips bicolorana*) and dotted rustic (*Rhyacia simulans*). Uncommon beetles (e.g. *Rhizophagus nitidulus*) and flies (e.g. *Stratiomys potamida*) have been found and it is certain that many uncommon insects remain to be discovered.

The hum and buzz of insect life is a wonderful feature of woodland in spring and summer. Insects play a vital role in the web of woodland life and the presence of large numbers of a wide range of insects indicates the ecological health of the wood. It is worth remembering that the presence of many insect-feeding birds, such as chiffchaff, blackcap and garden warbler, depend on insects as a food source.

Johnson's Piece

An open woodland on steeply sloping land to the south of Shotover Plain, Johnson's Piece has a few ancient oaks, and a range of mature deciduous and coniferous trees. Several thickets of scrub and young trees have invaded parts of the woodland. Open areas between trees are dominated by bracken. Spring-fed streams drain to the low point of the woodland and alongside these streams several attractive marshy areas have developed.

Post Royal Forest history On the nineteenth century sale maps[46,47] Johnson's Piece, then named Middle Ground, is described as rough grazing and furze. Indeed there is an old drinking trough which provides further evidence that the field was formerly grazed. In 1908 Rev. A.H. Johnson, a fellow of All Soul's College, along with a number of other members of Oxford University, subscribed to buy Johnson's Piece as a gift for the Chancellor, Masters and Scholars of the University of Oxford. Conditions of the gift were that the area should be devoted to the use of the public forever and that the charge of the land should be entrusted to the Curators of the University Parks[48]. Immediately after the land was entrusted to the University several ornamental trees were planted including sweet chestnut, sugar maple, red-leaved maple, Scots pine and Austrian pine, which have since matured to give the area something of the feel of an informal arboretum. In Church[49] there is a photograph taken in 1922 of Johnson's Piece, then named University Enclosure, which clearly shows how much more open the area was at that time. The 1947 aerial photograph[23] shows that there was less woodland there than now and it also shows the considerable erosion in the north caused by passage of military vehicles.

Wildlife The perimeter of Johnson's Piece is lined with ancient, pollarded oaks growing on an earthbank. A particularly ancient oak tree, the oldest on Shotover, is to be found at the north-east corner of the wood. One can only guess at the age of the tree but it could be as old as 300 years, and hence may have been living when Shotover was a royal forest. The wood is dominated by pedunculate oak, ash and silver birch. Apart from the exotic species mentioned in the previous section, other interesting species include common white beam, bird cherry and wild service tree, and saplings of all three species are found nearby. These three trees are native and could be indigenous to Shotover. However, bird cherry has a northerly and westerly distribution in England and it is likely that it was planted by Oxford University in the early 1900s.

The ground flora is sparse with only bluebells (*Hyacinthoides non-scripta*), red campion (*Silene dioica*), yellow pimpernel (*Lysimachia nemorum*) and greater stichwort (*Stellaria holostea*) breaking the domination by tall stands of bracken (*Pteridium aquilinum*). More interesting plants are found in the marshy areas which are described elsewhere.

Johnson's Piece – mixed deciduous woodland

Magdalen Wood

Magdalen Wood has closely spaced oaks which have not achieved the height or girth of Brasenose Wood's trees. The most substantial of Magdalen Wood's trees are Scots pine and Austrian pine which were planted in 1892 close to the buildings of Wood Farm (now destroyed). There is a sparse shrub layer in the wood and the ground layer is dominated by brambles.

Post Royal Forest history Between the seventeenth and nineteenth centuries Magdalen Wood was let on a series of seven year leases. In Mr. North's lease of 1766 for example[52], the rent for seven years was £14 but all the timber from the woodland was reserved for College use. At the end of the eighteenth and beginning of the nineteenth centuries trees from Magdalen Wood were used to repair the buildings of Wood Farm[53], but the paucity of records of timber sales suggests that Magdalen Wood was not as important a source of timber as some other parts of Shotover Forest. Although no longer subject to forest laws there were still severe penalties for misdemeanors in local woodland. In March 1766 Edward Jones was publicly whipped for stealing two faggots from Magdalen Wood[54]. In 1872 there was a court case concerning rights of ingress and egress through Magdalen Wood[55], and the accompanying text and map afford an insight into the condition of Wood Farm in the nineteenth century. Open Magdalen was described as having some timber trees with brakes of thorns, briars and furze. The dispute concerned the people of Cowley who had common grazing rights on Elder Stubs. Before inclosure (1853) parishioners were in the habit of taking their cattle through Open Magdalen on their way to graze on Elder Stubs, and of taking their cattle back through Open Brasenose. The dispute continued for about 40 years with Magdalen College fencing the wood and erecting a gate to prevent the entrance of cattle, and the local farmers breaking down the gate and firing the furze on Open Magdalen. In 1893 a second prosecution was brought against two locals, the famous Oxford botanist George Claridge Druce being a witness for the prosecution. The result was that the parishioners sold Elder Stubs and purchased a recreation ground within the parish of Cowley[56]. Wood Farm was sold to Oxford Corporation in the 1930s, and most of the land is now used for housing apart from Open Magdalen, which is now known as Magdalen Wood.

Wildlife Dominated by a close canopy of pedunculate oak, Magdalen Wood has no old trees to compare with the mature stems of Brasenose Wood. Other trees present include silver birch, yew, turkey oak, larch, Scots pine and Austrian pine. The trees of Magdalen Wood are mostly of uniform age and date from the end of the nineteenth century. The lack of any thinning operations has resulted in a shortage of quality timber trees.

Magdalen Wood – young oaks with hazel understorey

The ground flora of Magdalen Wood is depauperate compared to that of the neighbouring Brasenose Wood. Brambles dominate but a few woodland flowers such as wood anemone (*Anemone nemorosa*), lesser celandine (*Ranunculus ficaria*), wood spurge (*Euphorbia amygdaloides*), wood sorrel (*Oxalis acetosella*), bluebell (*Hyacinthoides non-scripta*) and hairy-brome (*Bromus ramosus*) are found. It will be interesting to see whether the woodland is colonized by further woodland plants from Brasenose Wood. Magdalen Wood is not an ancient wood and it provides a good example of the differences which can exist between neighbouring and superficially similar woods. Both woods are dominated by oak and lie on similar soils. The marked differences in flora result from the different histories of the two woods.

Sydling's and Wick Copse

A rich and varied woodland is found on the steeply sloping gulley sides of the stream draining westwards through Sydling's Copse. Some splendid oaks with a rich understorey grow on the southern slope at the eastern end – the northern slope at this end is a sweet chestnut and Scots pine plantation. Downstream the ancient oak woodland is replaced by a mosaic of oak, ash, birch and hawthorn trees interspersed by reed-dominated wetland clearings.

Post Royal Forest history Following disafforestation Sydling's Copse was owned by Brasenose College and it remained in their possession until 1978 when it was sold to the local naturalists' trust (BBONT) who manage the wood as a nature reserve. A good deal of tree planting took place at Sydling's Copse during the Second World War when a number of exotic softwood and hardwood species were introduced. However, the oak standard and hazel coppice woodland was relatively unaffected by the planting regime.

Wick Copse and College Pond were owned by Christ Church College after disafforestation and most of the area remains in the College's ownership. However, since 1975 most of the area has been leased to BBONT. Consequently both Sydling's Copse, and Wick Copse and College Pond are managed as nature reserves. An exception is a part of Wick Copse on the south side of the stream which passed into private ownership. It is unfortunate that the management of this small area has been unsympathetic to the wildlife and pollution from continued rubbish dumping threatens the integrity of the western end of the valley.

Wildlife A fine stretch of ancient woodland runs along the south side of the gulley formed by the stream which runs west through Sydling's and Wick Copse. Some magnificent oaks are a feature of this wood – other trees include wild cherry, rowan, silver birch and field maple. The presence of beech and larch result from recent plantings. A rich and varied coppice layer includes hazel, blackthorn, hawthorn, and dogwood, with wayfaring-tree, guelder-rose, buckthorn and spindle on the southern edge.

The herb layer is particularly attractive with abundant stands of dog's mercury (*Mercurialis perennis*), wood anemone (*Anemone nemorosa*), bluebell (*Hyacinthoides non-scripta*) and yellow archangel (*Lamiastrum galeobdelon*). Several more local species are also present including herb-Paris (*Paris quadrifolia*), ramsons (*Allium ursinum*), nettle-leaved bellflower (*Campanula trachelium*), toothwort (*Lathraea squamaria*) and early purple-orchid (*Orchis mascula*).

Many interesting and attractive fungi grow in this area of woodland. Spring-fruiting fungi of note are the scarlet elf cup (*Sarcoscypha coccinea*) and morel (*Morchella esculenta*). Autumn fruiting species include wood blewit (*Lepista nuda*), earth star (*Geastrum rufescens*) and magpie fungus (*Coprinus picaceus*). The very distinctive bird's-nest fungus (*Crucibulum vulgare*) may be found here in most months of the year.

Many mammals live in the valley. An extensive badger's set occurs in the woodland and badgers may be seen at dusk in spring and summer. Indeed their prints are often seen in the winter's snow which suggests that badgers do not sleep throughout the winter. Muntjac are regularly seen in the wood and the larger slots of fallow deer have been noted on occasions. Foxes have their earths in this woodland bank. Small rodents such as bank vole, wood mouse and shrew undoubtedly occur although no detailed survey has been made.

A wide range of birds nest in the woodland. All three British wood-peckers breed here as do several other hole nesting species such as blue tit, great tit, marsh tit, starling, stock dove and tawny owl. A wide range of summer migrant warblers nest in the brambles and undergrowth of the wooded slopes. Many nest boxes have been erected in this woodland. It is interesting to note that even in mature woodland with many natural tree holes, next boxes are always used by birds. The nest boxes seem to provide a '5-star' nesting site which is probably drier and less draughty than the natural holes.

The invertebrate life of the woodland is rich but little known. Butterflies present include white admiral and purple hairstreak. Until the late 1970s a flourishing colony of white-letter hairstreaks occurred in the woods. However, the caterpillars are elm feeders and so their source of food (wych elm) vanished with the onset of Dutch Elm disease. This charming butter-fly is now thought to have become extinct in the wood. Indeed virtually all mature elms have disappeared from Oxfordshire and it is possible that the white-letter hairstreak will be lost from the county.

Several interesting moths occur in the woodland including the orange underwing (*Archiearis parthenias*), archer's dart (*Agrotis vestigialis*), green arches (*Anaplectoides prasina*) and pale eggar (*Trichiura crataegi*).

A final group of invertebrates which has been studied in some detail is the molluscs. Snails depend on the presence of limestone from the Coral Rag to build up their shells. Interesting species which have been found include *Ena montana, E. obscura* and *Acicula fusca. Ena montana* is a rare

southern species found in ancient woodland on calcareous soils.

Noke Wood and Cooke's Copse

Situated on the slope leading down to Otmoor, Noke Wood provides some extensive views over the moor. Cooke's Copse has a canopy of mature beech with little understorey. Springs arise in the copse which produce areas of wetland supporting some interesting plants such as golden saxifrage. Noke Wood is an attractive woodland with many mature trees, a rich understorey and a remarkable display of woodland flowers in spring. Other notable features include several small streams, which drain down a bank which slopes to the north, and a broad, grassy ride alongside a conifer plantation.

Post Royal Forest history Noke Wood (formerly known as Oke and meaning 'at the oak trees') has been in private ownership for many centuries. Following the Second World War substantial areas of the central part of the wood were planted with poplars and conifers. These plantations have been actively maintained and indeed the understorey has been coppiced in the 1980s and some replanting with oak and beech carried out. Pheasants are reared in the wood. Cooke's Copse is dominated by mature beech and presumably does not have the same history of woodland continuity as Noke Wood.

Wildlife Ramsons (*Allium ursinum*), violet helleborine (*Epipactis purpurata*) and opposite-leaved golden saxifrage (*Chrysosplenium oppositifolium*) are found in Cooke's Copse, which has little understorey under mature beech trees.

The trees and shrubs of the seminatural stands are rich and similar to those found in Sydling's Copse and Brasenose Wood. Herbaceous species of note include wild daffodil (*Narcissus pseudonarcissus*), early purple-orchid (*Orchis mascula*), spurge laurel (*Daphne laureola*), yellow pimpernel (*Lysimachia nemorum*) and water avens (*Geum rivale*).

Woodeaton Wood

On gently sloping ground to the east of the river Cherwell, Woodeaton Wood is a splendid 15 ha oak woodland, with large oak and ash trees and a rich understorey and herbaceous layer. A small stream drains through the wood and eventually into the Cherwell. Little woodland management has been carried out in recent years, giving the wood a rather 'closed-in' character.

Post Royal Forest history A feature of Woodeaton Wood is the shortage of introduced tree species. However, a few exotic trees have been

Woodeaton Wood – neglected coppice with stream

planted in the wood including white poplar and Norway spruce, of which
five mature trees remain. Some clearance has been undertaken in recent
years associated with a wired-off pheasant release pen, but in general little
management activity has occurred and many of the paths are overgrown.

Wildlife Oak standards predominate but there are a few large ash
arising from stools and other trees present include field maple, sycamore,
aspen and wild cherry. The full range of Shotover shrubs is present including the calcicolous wayfaring-tree, guelder-rose and spindle.

Herbaceous plants are exceptionally diverse with a wide range of woodland species including several which are locally uncommon – wild daffodil
(*Narcissus pseudonarcissus*), herb-Paris (*Paris quadrifolia*), an abundance
of water avens (*Geum rivale*), meadow saffron (*Colchicum autumnale*),
stinking iris (*Iris foetidissima*), early purple-orchid (*Orchis mascula*),
ramsons (*Allium ursinum*) and nettle-leaved bellflower (*Campanula
trachelium*).

Holly Wood

A pleasing wood which is largely seminatural in character, Holly Wood
does have a small area of conifers but is dominated by some good-sized
oak timber trees with a rich shrub layer. A feature of the wood is the relatively open areas caused by recently coppiced underwood sections. Sallows
have been planted as a conservation measure by a sympathetic owner, to
encourage the purple emperor butterfly.

Post Royal Forest history Although well separated from the core
of the Royal Forest, Holly Wood is included in the thirteenth century
perambulation as Hornle[7]. In the early 1700s the present day Holly Wood
was known as Lower Horley Wood. In addition an Upper Horley or Gogmire
Wood adjoined Lower Horley to the north-west. Gogmire Wood is known to
have been standing in 1856 but it has now been felled and the land is used
for arable farming. Holly Wood has been in private ownership for many
centuries.

Wildlife A small percentage of the wood has been planted with
alien poplars and conifers – larch, Scots pine and Norway spruce. There are
many old trees in the wood with pedunculate oak predominating. An aspen
clone is growing close to the southern boundary. Although in many ways
Holly Wood is like the other Shotover woods, there is one notable difference. Wild cherry, which is common in the other Shotover woods, is very
scarce in Holly Wood.

The full range of shrub species occur in Holly Wood including Midland
hawthorn, spindle, holly and guelder-rose. A regime of coppice cutting is
in operation and there is every indication that as in Brasenose Wood, this
traditional form of woodland management has continued for many years.

Page 67: Holly Wood – main ride
Pages 68 – 69: Stanton Great Wood – mixed oak woodland with wide, well-maintained rides

A good range of herbaceous species is present including early purple-orchid (*Orchis mascula*), goldilocks (*Ranunculus auricomus*), ramsons (*Allium ursinum*) and two sedges, pale sedge (*Carex pallescens*) and pendulous sedge (*C. pendula*), which are absent from most other Shotover woods. Primroses (*Primula vulgaris*) and bluebells (*Hyacinthoides non-scripta*) grow in profusion on the bank alongside Holly Lane and make a colourful display in springtime. Two rare butterflies breed in Holly Wood – the black hairstreak, which is confined to substantial blackthorn thickets, and the purple emperor, whose caterpillars feed on sallow leaves.

Stanton Great Wood

A substantial wood of 60 ha, half the area of Stanton Great Wood is now devoted to conifers. The areas of deciduous woodland are attractive and reminiscent of Holly Wood, with a good cover of mature oaks which may date from the First World War. A striking feature of the woodland is the abundance of wild service trees. The coniferous sections are actively main-tained and the forestry programme has resulted in many openings and glades within the wood.

Post Royal Forest history Stanton Great Wood is situated close to Holly Wood in the parish of Stanton St. John. Mentioned in the 1298 perambulation as *Sydele*, Stanton Great Wood was called Sidley Wood or St. John's Wood in the early 1700s[7], when it was known to have been divided into a number of compartments for the purpose of maintaining a coppicing regime. More recently about half of the wood has been planted with conifers. Some areas of coppice are regularly cut in the hardwood sections, but the density of standards has reduced underwood regrowth.

Wildlife In many ways Stanton Great Wood is much more similar to Holly Wood, with the same trees and shrubs, than to the other Shotover woods. An important difference is that there are many fine wild service trees in the wood. The ground flora is not as rich as in Holly Wood, with pale sedge (*Carex pallescens*) being one of the most interesting species.

Long Wood

West of Woodeaton Wood, Long Wood is clearly an ancient piece of wood-land although it is not mentioned by name in the early documents. The presence of the full range of Shotover's trees and shrubs in Long Wood indicates its antiquity. However, the herbaceous species are not as varied as in the larger woods but plants found include primrose (*Primula vulgaris*), wood spurge (*Euphorbia amygdaloides*), wood anemone (*Anemone nemorosa*) and water avens (*Geum rivale*).

Other woods

In addition to the predominantly seminatural woodlands discussed hitherto, several additional woods occur within the bounds of Shotover Royal Forest which have changed so substantially as to bear little resemblance to their former state. Some woodland plants are able to survive considerable changes in their environment. The Spinney on the north side of Shotover Hill bears little resemblance to a seminatural woodland, having substantial stands of conifers, sycamore and beech. The wood is bisected by a cascade of artificial ponds, constructed originally for trout raising. These woods have considerable natural history interest with locally uncommon plants such as soft shield-fern (*Polystichum setiferum*), lady fern (*Athyrium filix-femina*), wood speedwell (*Veronica montana*), spurge laurel (*Daphne laureola*) and the local thin-spiked wood sedge (*Carex strigosa*). Several dragon- and damselflies have been seen on the ponds including *Libellula quadrimaculata*, *Sympetrum striolatum*, *Aeshna juncea*, *Coenagrion puella* and *Ischnura elegans*, and birds such as moorhen, dabchick, mallard, kingfisher and grey wagtail have been seen.

Stowood, although a mere shadow of its former self having lost species such as columbine (*Aquilegia vulgaris*), meadow saxifrage (*Saxifraga granulata*) and nettle-leaved bellflower (*Campanula trachelium*), still retains some interest. The fringe of hazel coppice along the north and west boundaries is attractive with plants such as ramsons (*Allium ursinum*), primrose (*Primula vulgaris*), moschatel (*Adoxa moschatellina*), wood anemone (*Anemone nemorosa*), sweet violet (*Viola odorata*) and red currant (*Ribes rubrum*). Hares, which are in decline in the Oxford area, are still to be seen in the wood and the surrounding arable fields.

Chapter 9

Conservation

We have seen that the area of seminatural wildlife habitats has declined by more than 90% since royal forest times. The remaining 8% or so which is seminatural provides the most attractive and interesting part of Shotover's countryside. Being so close to Oxford, Shotover is appreciated by many people in terms of providing peaceful places in which to walk, an attractive landscape feature and interesting study sites for school children and students.

Partly because of such proximity to Oxford, there are bound to be future pressures to develop Shotover's countryside in one way or another. In recent decades the Bayswater meadow has been ploughed, two areas of seminatural woodland have been severely damaged by illegal dumping of rubbish and an area of grassland and woodland has been threatened with the introduction of a local authority gypsy encampment. In order to ensure the future survival of Shotover's best countryside it is necessary firstly to document what remains and to stop any detrimental development, and secondly to provide suggestions for wise management – both aspects are covered by the term conservation.

No existing area of seminatural vegetation should be allowed to change in any way which could adversely affect the wildlife. Shotover's finest woods have taken 10,000 years to mature into what they are now and so replacement is a lengthy process. Because there is so little top quality Shotover countryside left and because replacement takes so long, that which remains must be conserved at all costs. Some of the best quality woodlands (Sydling's Copse and College Pond, Woodeaton Wood, Brasenose Wood, Holly Wood and Stanton Great Wood) receive a degree of protection because they are designated Sites of Special Scientific Interest (SSSIs) under which the owners are advised on management by the Nature Conservancy Council (NCC) and a range of damaging operations forbidden without prior consultation. Three of the woods (Sydling's Copse, Henry Stephen/C.S. Lewis reserve and Shotover Spinney) are managed as nature reserves and hence receive extra protection. About half of Shotover's good quality wildlife habitat is within Shotover Country Park – an amenity area owned by Oxford City Council. Most of the rest of Shotover receives some protection from the planning procedures whereby the building of houses or industrial premises is strictly controlled. But this is not enough. Only a real appreciation of the importance of Shotover's countryside by members of the public and great vigilance can hope to ensure that none of it is damaged or destroyed.

A second aspect of conservation is the wise management of existing high quality countryside. None of the habitats described earlier will maintain their interest without substantial intervention by man. It is something of a paradox that virtually all of the countryside of inland, lowland

England would change dramatically in a few decades without the intervention of man. It is possible to make a few general rules for the wise management of Shotover's countryside.

Grassland is best maintained by light grazing and/or hay cutting. Shotover Hill's acid grassland has deteriorated following the cessation of agricultural grazing in the 1930s and the reduction of rabbit grazing following the arrival of myxomatosis in 1954. Surrounding limestone grassland has almost all been ploughed. The only hope for limestone grassland is for a sympathetic owner to cease arable usage and to replace with a low intensity grazing regime. Practices which are likely to damage existing seminatural grasslands are ploughing and reseeding, fertilizing and the application of pesticides.

The area of heathland, a rare habitat in Oxfordshire, could be increased by management aimed at reducing the cover of woody plants and bracken. Traditionally heathland was managed by grazing or burning. However, it will be necessary first to reduce the bracken cover before the traditional management techniques can be re-employed.

Of the wetland habitats, fen and marsh can be maintained by period-

Small copse of ancient woodland near Elsfield damaged by illegal rubbish tipping

ically reducing the cover of woody plants, by controlling excessive trampling and by locally raising the water table. As with ponds, water purity is vital and so agricultural chemicals should not be allowed to run into water courses. With the ponds some emergent vegetation is important and islands provide nesting cover for birds. Most of Shotover's ponds have a tendency to silt up which needs to be controlled. Surrounding trees and shrubs must be cut from time to time to allow sunlight to reach at least the south side of the ponds, and to reduce the input of leaves which may lead to eutrophication.

Few people realise that woodlands in lowland England require management to maintain the wildlife interest. The introduction of a forestry programme involving regular light felling and regular replanting is desirable. The aim of the felling should be to result in a stand of trees of all ages, from very young to very old, and to ensure that within this constraint the maximum timber potential is realised. Replanting should only be with indigenous stock – Shotover woodlands should be maintained with Shotover oaks. A substantial network of rides is desirable and these rides should be actively maintained to encourage the shrubby ride edges and

Recently bulldozed woodland near Stowood (1983)

their associated light-loving plants. Details of woodland management will vary from wood to wood, but in coppice-with-standard woods such as Brasenose and Holly Woods, it is important to retain the traditional coppice cutting regime.

Certain factors affecting Shotover's wildlife are out of the control of local people. An example is air pollution from the Cowley factories which has an adverse effect. SO_2 emission from the factory chimneys is probably the main culprit but there are other pollutants such as the noxious, aromatic compounds occasionally released from the British Leyland paint shops. There is an increasing awareness throughout the western world of the harm caused by insidious air pollutants such as SO_2 which has recently given rise to the term 'acid rain'. It is possible that in future years stronger legislation will be introduced to reduce air pollution, which will ensure that increased filtering will reduce gaseous emissions. Should our air be made cleaner by law it will be interesting to note the effect on Shotover's wildlife. It is certain that the effect will be beneficial and in particular the epiphyte flora will improve both in abundance and variety.

Let us hope that the future is rosy for Shotover's countryside. We cannot afford to lose any of the remaining seminatural habitats and all of the countryside needs to be wisely managed for the wildlife.

Appendix 1

Perambulation of Shotover and Stowood Forest (c.1298)

(Translated by Ernest Black from the account in the Boarstall Cartulary)

The Bounds of Shotover and Stowood Forest

In the same way the jurors say that the forest of Shotover begins at the mill which is called Sotelescote mill, [Sescut Farm by the Cherwell], and in this way along the ditch which is between the estate of our lord the king of Hedyngdone and the land of John Ellesfeld, with the inclusion of the forest on the right hand along all the bounds and boundary marks recorded below and by leaving outside the forest on the left side all the remainder; and in this way as far as stonybrigge; and in this way along the ditch as far as Edenbroke [Bayswater Brook?], and in this way as far as the boundary mark which is called Ensingrovemere, which is between the field of Ellesfeld and the field of Wyke [Wick]; and in this way as far as Stodefold [a field which flanked the boundary between Wick and Elsfield]; and in this way as far as the Brech; and in this way as far as the Brechhurne which is between the wood of our master the king which is called Stowode [Stowood] and the Brech of Ellesfeld; and so along the ditch as far as Eldendone; and so as far as Bytheweyesende; and so as far as Becklelestyle; and so through the pasture as far as hangerescade through the wood of Ellesfeld; and in this way between the wood of Wodetone [Woodeaton] and Stowode [Stowood] as far as Kyngeshoke; and so as far as Dudesweyesend near the lake which is called Wodetonehoo; and so as far as Longerudyngesende which is between Stowode and Cowaliz [a now lost 720 acre wood near Islip], and so as far as Bradenbrigg; and so as far as Thremeren between Stowode and the wood of Henry Tyeys [Noke Wood] and the wood of the abbot of Westminster and as far as the corner of Parkeres brech de Beckele; and so as far as Dichende de Beckele; and so straight through the pasture of Beckele as far as Stowode mere; and so as far as Beckelehache; and so through the pasture as far as Bantereshale; and so through the pasture as far as the Brecheshurne to the highest point of the wood of John of St. John and so as far as the Meresthorn between the arable land of Stantone [Stanton St. John] and Wyke [Wick]; and so as far as Bardescroft of Stoford [a hamlet at the extreme south west of Stanton St. John]; and so along the boundary ditch of the slated croft as far as the bridge of Stoford, and so along the boundary ditch between the arable land of Hedyngdone and the arable land of Forsthull [Forest Hill]; and as far as Sanden [Sandhills]; and so along the boundary ditch between the arable land of Forsthull and Shotover as far as Lynhale [Studley Priory's wood known to have been felled prior to 1670]; and so as far as Byondebroke between the wood of our lord the king and the wood of Forsthull; and so as far as Wodemanneshull; and so as far as Farnewellebroke beside Grovesende; and so as far as Halenghtonehache [a small quarry]; and so as far as Mintehale; and so as far as Baustakebroke Netherende; and so along the boundary ditch as far as Kyngeswodebroke; and so as far as the lower end of Akemere next to Kyngeswodebroke as far as the Redediche, by climbing up to the wood of the Temple and so by descending through the wood of the Temple as far as Mereweye, which lies next to Shotover; and so as far as Akermerebroke, and as far as the aforementioned Rededych between the wood of John of Scaccario and the wood of the Temple as far as Redychesheued; and so by going downhill as far as Akermerwelle; and so as far as the track next to the wood of Shotover; and so along the track between the wood of Shotover and Horspathe and so to the summit of Akermere; and so as far as Chalfle along the boundary hedge between Peryhale [a wood to the south east of present day Open Brasenose] and Chalfle; and so as far as the royal road which leads towards Oxford; and so along the same road as far as the small bridge [Magdalen Bridge] of Oxford; and so as far as Charwelle [Cherwell] as far as the mill which is called Sotelescotemulle etc.

And the aforesaid jurors state that the wood of Ellesfeld which now belongs to John of Ellesfeld and the wood of Woodeaton which is held by the abbot of Eynsham, and the wood of Cowaliz which is held by the abbot of Westminster, and the wood of Oke which is held by Henry

Tyeys, and the wood of Forsthull which is held by the abbot of Osney and the Prioress of Studely, and the wood of Shawe which is held by the abbot of Abingdon, and the wood of Horspath which is held by the master of the knights of the Temple in England and the wood of Chalfle which is held by the same master of the knights, and the woods of Hornle [Holly] and of Sydele [Stanton Great Wood] in Stanton which are held by John of St. John, were brought within the forest after the coronation of the lord King Henry the great grandfather of our present lord king with this condition, that neither they (those named above) nor their predecessors or earlier owners after a stated time up till now were able to remove anything from the aforesaid woods except through the dispensation of the foresters and as the same foresters wish, nor should they be able to take anything else of use from the same woods, just as they were accustomed to have and to do before the time of the coronation of our lord King Henry the aforesaid and by the attachment and hindrance of the aforesaid foresters. And they state that all the aforesaid woods were afforested after the coronation of the lord King Henry the greatgrandfather of our lord the present king just as they have understood and understand from the report of their predecessors and of other honest men and through the general repute of their predecessors and through all the villages lying close to the same forest.

Natural History

The catalogue of plant and animal species from Shotover is far from complete and there remains a great deal to be found. Of the studies that have been made some areas have received much more attention than others. The plants and animals of Sydling's Copse and Brasenose Wood are much better known than the other Shotover woods. This uneven approach is in part due to accessibility – the majority of Shotover woods are in private hands and access is only possible along public footpaths. However, the inclusion of all available information seems sensible and may be of value for comparison in future years.

Key to Appendices

* Species not recorded since 1980
(1874 Baxter) Date of last known record and recorder
Numbers **1-17** which follow species names refer to the following places

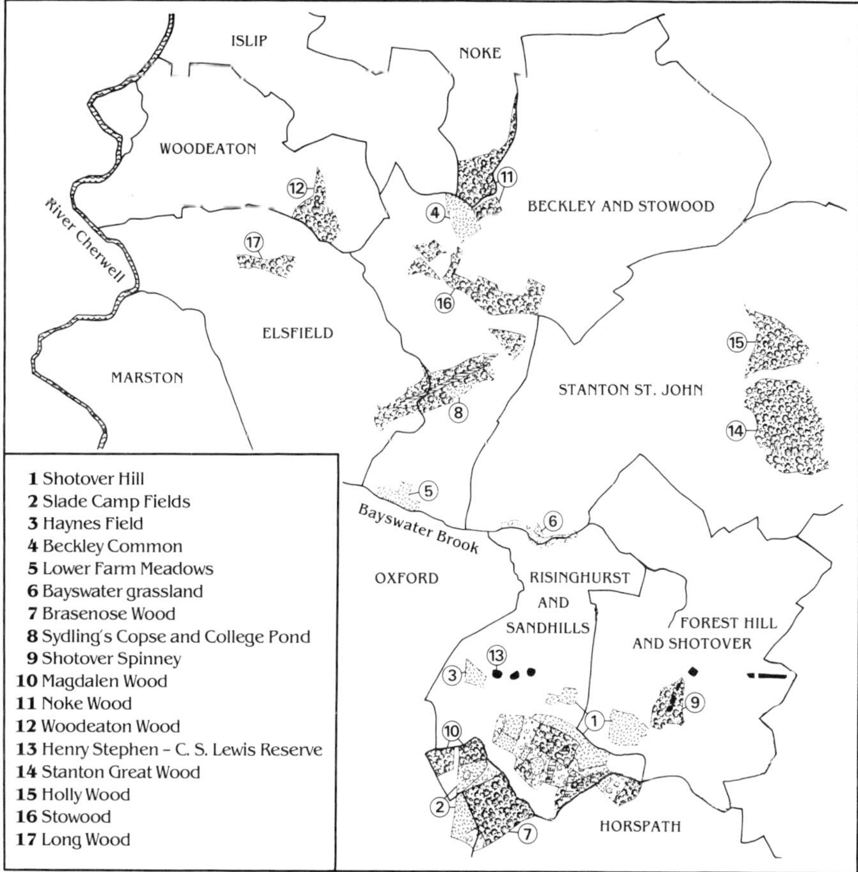

1 Shotover Hill
2 Slade Camp Fields
3 Haynes Field
4 Beckley Common
5 Lower Farm Meadows
6 Bayswater grassland
7 Brasenose Wood
8 Sydling's Copse and College Pond
9 Shotover Spinney
10 Magdalen Wood
11 Noke Wood
12 Woodeaton Wood
13 Henry Stephen – C. S. Lewis Reserve
14 Stanton Great Wood
15 Holly Wood
16 Stowood
17 Long Wood

Appendix 2

Bryophytes

A wide range of mosses and liverworts has been recorded from Shotover. Of particular interest is the fact that several early botanists visited Shotover, and Jacob Bobart (1641-1719) made some of the world's earliest bryophyte collections there. John Sibthorp (1758-96) and William Baxter (1787-1871) also collected at Shotover.

Many mosses and liverworts are very exacting in their habitat requirements. For this reason the known loss of many bryophytes provides an indication of ecological changes which have taken place. The known extinction of a community of bryophytes including *Sphagnum subnitens, S. squarrosum, S. palustre, Polytrichum commune, Dicranum bonjeani, Splachnum ampullaceum, Philonotis fontana, Riccardia sinuata, Cephalozia connivens* and *Lepidozia setacea* testifies to the total of peat bog from Shotover. Heath and acid grassland, which have many bryophytes in common, have lost *Pogonatum nanum, P. aloides, Racomitrium canescens, Bryum pseudo-triquetrum, Nardia scalaris* and *Solenostoma crenulatum.*

Shotover's epiphyte flora is depauperate and known extinctions include *Orthotrichum striatum, Ulota phyllantha, Cryphaea heteromalla, Leucodon sciouroides* and *Radula complanata.* There are several possible reasons for the epiphyte extinctions but it could well be that the increased level of SO_2 in the atmosphere is the main culprit.

Species such as *Anthoceros punctatus* and *Ephemerum serratum* have been lost from the arable fields and others such as *Acaulon muticum* only remain in minute quantities. The reason for these losses is probably the change in farming practices which has resulted in arable fields being cultivated throughout the year and not being left fallow for any length of time.

ANTHOCEROTALES
* *Anthoceros punctatus* (W. Baxter)
MARCHANTIALES
Lunularia cruciata **1**
Conocephalum conicum **1, 8**
Marchantia polymorpha **1**
Riccia glauca **1**
METZGERIALES
* *Riccardia sinuata* **1** (19th century)
R. pinguis **8**
Pellia epiphylla **1, 8**
P. fabbroniana **1, 8**
Metzgeria furcata **1, 8**
* *Fossombronia pusilla* **1** (Sibthorp)
JUNGERMANNIALES
* *Lophozia incisa* **1** (1819 Baxter)
* *Lepidozia reptans* **1** (1948 E. W. Jones)
* *L. setacea* **1** (19th century)
Calypogeia fissa **1, 8**
* *Solenostoma crenulata* **1** (Baxter)
Plagiochila asplenioides **7, 8**
* *Nardia scalaris* **1** (1940's E. W. Jones)
Lophocolea bidentata **1, 7**
L. cuspidata **1, 7**
L. heterophylla **1, 7, 8**
Chiloscyphus pallescens **7, 8**
Cephalozia bicuspidata **1**
* *C. connivens* **1** (1819 Baxter)
* *Diplophyllum albicans* **1** (Baxter)
* *Scapania nemorea* **1** (1819 Baxter)
* *Radula complanata* **1** (Sibthorp)
SPHAGNALES
* *Sphagnum subnitens* **1**
* *S. squarrosum* **1**
* *S. palustre* **1**

POLYTRICHALES
Tetraphis pellucida **8**
Atrichum undulatum **7, 8**
Polytrichum formosum **1, 8**
* *P. commune* **1** (lost in about 1861)
P. juniperinum **1**
* *Pogonatum nanum* **1** (Sibthorp)
* *P. aloides* **1** (Sibthorp)
DICRANALES
Pleuridium acuminatum **1, 7**
* *P. subulatum* **1**
Ceratodon purpureus **1, 7, 8**
Dicranella varia **1**
D. heteromalla **1, 8**
* *D. cerviculata* **1** (Sibthorp)
Dicranoweissia cirrata **1, 7, 8**
Dicranum scoparium **1, 8**
* *D. bonjeani* **1** (Baxter)
D. tauricum (=*strictum*) **7**

Polytrichum formosum

Bryophytes

Campylopus pyriformis **1, 8**
* *C. flexuosus* **1** (Baxter)
C. introflexus **8**
FISSIDENTALES
Fissidens bryoides **1, 8**
F. adianthoides **8**
F. cristatus **8**
F. taxifolius **1, 8**
F. viridulus **8**
* *F. exilis* **1** (1940's E. W. Jones)
F. incurvus **8**
ENCALYPTALES
* *Encalypta vulgaris* (Sibthorp)
POTTIALES
Tortula ruralis **1, 7**
T. intermedia **7**
T. muralis **1, 7, 8**
* *T. subulata* **1** (Sibthorp)
* *Aloina aloides* **1**
Acaulon muticum **8** small quantities 1979
Pottia truncata **1**
P. lanceolata **1**
P. bryoides **8**
P. starkeana ssp. conica **1**
P. minutula **8**
Phascum cuspidatum **8**
Barbula unguiculata **1**
B. rigidula **1**
B. cylindrica **1, 7, 8**
B. convoluta **8**
* *B. fallax* **1**
* *B. tophacea* **1**
B. recurvirostra **8**
* *Weissia microstoma* **1**
Oxystegus sinuosus **8**
GRIMMIALES
Schistidium (=Grimmia) apocarpum **2**
Grimmia pulvinata **2**
* *Racomitrium canescens* **1** (extinct by 1856 – Sibthorp)
FUNARIALES
Funaria hygrometrica **1, 7, 8**
* *Physcomitrium pyriforme* (1940's E. W. Jones)
* *Ephemerum serratum* **1**
* *Sphachnum ampullaceum* **1** (1819)
BRYALES
Orthodontium lineare **1, 8**
Bryum pallens **7**
* *B. turbinatum* **1**
B. argenteum **7**
* *B. pseudotriquetrum* **1** (Sibthorp)
B. rubens **7, 8**
* *B. affine* **1** (Baxter)
B. bicolor **7**
B. flaccidum **8**
* *B. intermedium* **1**
B. capillare **1, 7, 8**
* *B. erythrocarpum*
B. microerythrocarpum **8**
* *Rhodobryum roseum* **1** (Sibthorp)
Pohlia carnea (=deliculata) **1, 7**
P. nutans **1, 7, 8**
* *P. wahlenbergii* **1** (1858)

Mnium hornum **1, 7, 8**
* *M. cuspidatum* **1** (Sibthorp)
Plagiomnium (=Mnium) undulatum **1, 8**
P. rostratum **8**
P. affine **8**
Rhizomnium (=Mnium) punctatum **1, 8**
Aulacomnium androgynum **1, 7**
* *A. palustre* **1** (1884)
* *Philonotis fontana* **1** (Sibthorp)
ISOBRYALES
Homalia trichomaniodes **8**
Thamnobryum (=Thamnium) alopecurum **7, 8**
Climacium dendroides **8**
* *Cryphaea heteromalla* **1** (Baxter)
* *Leucodon sciuroides* **1** (Sibthorp)
ORTHOTRICHALES
Zygodon viridissimus **8**
* *Orthotrichum anomalum* **1** (Sibthorp)
* *O. striatum* (Baxter)
O. affine **8** on elder
* *Ulota phyllantha* **1**
U. crispa **8** very small quantities
HYPNOBRYALES
Cratoneuron filicinum **8**
C. commutatum **8**
Pseudoscleropodium purum **1, 2, 7, 8**
Campylium protensum **8**
Amblystegium serpens **1, 8**
* *A. varium* **1**
Homalothecium (=Camptothecium) sericeum **1, 7**
Drepanocladus revolvens **8**
D. uncinatus **8**
Calliergon cuspidatum **8**
* *C. cordifolium* **1**
Isothecium myosuroides **7**
I. myurum **1, 8**
Bracythecium albicans **1**
B. velutinum **1, 7, 8**
B. rutabulum **1, 7, 8**
Rhyncostegium (=Eurhynchium) confertum **7**
* *R. riparoides* **8**
Eurhynchium praelongum **1, 7, 8**
* *E. pumilum* **1** (1940's E. W. Jones)
E. striatum **8**
E. swartzii **8**
E. murale **8**
Cirriphylum pilliferum **7, 8**
* *Isopterygium elegans* **1** (1940's E. W. Jones)
Plagiothecium nemorale **1, 8**
P. denticulatum **8**
P. ruthei **8**
Hypnum cupressiforme **1, 7, 8**
H. mammillatum **8**
Ctenidium molluscum **8**
Pleurozium schreberi **1**
Rhytidiadelphus squarrosus **7, 8**
* *R. lorens* **1** (Sibthorp)

* Species not recorded since 1980.
Moss nomenclature after Smith, A. J. E. (1978) The Moss
Flora of Britain and Ireland. C.U.P.
Liverwort nomenclature after Watson, E. V. (1968) British
Mosses and Liverworts. C.U.P.

Appendix 3

Lichens

Shotover's woodlands possess few lichen species compared to woods away from urban development. *Lecanora conizaeoides* occurs abundantly as a thick, grey-green crust on bark. The abundance of this pollution-tolerant lichen shows that Shotover's lichen flora is affected by atmospheric pollution.
L. conizaeoides is scarce in the pollution-free woodlands of western Britain, because of competition from some of the large, foliose lichens which are extremely sensitive to air pollution. *Cladonia coniocraea*, which grows at the base of many of Shotover's mature oaks, is often found with the moss *Hypnum cupressiforme*. A third woodland lichen association is based on *Hypogymnia physodes*, which is found in greatest abundance on large, horizontal branches of oak trees. Small quantities of *Evernia prunastri* and *Cetraria glauca* are found growing with *H. physodes*. These lichens do not survive in areas of severe atmospheric pollution and so they indicate that Shotover does not suffer as bad air pollution as some parts of the country.

The acid grassland and heath of Shotover Hill contain few lichens. However a careful search will reveal five species of *Cladonia; C. allosquamosa, C. chlorophaea, C. fimbriata, C. pyxidata* and *C. subulata.*

The limestone walls on Shotover possess a rich lichen flora which is more tolerant of atmospheric pollution than the woodland lichen flora. Species present include *Caloplaca citrina, C. heppiana, Dimerella lutea, Lecanora campestris, Physcia caesia, P. orbicularis, P. grisea* and *Xanthoria parietina.* The exposed, sandstone doggers have several species of lichen growing on them including *Bacidia umbrina, Candelariella vitellina, Lecanora dispersa, L. muralis* and *Physcia caesia.*

Lichens as indicators of pollution

It has been suggested that primeval deciduous forests of lowland Britain had about 150 species of lichen per km[2] and this is about the present day figure for the New Forest[58]. It is certainly true that the richest epiphytic lichen flora is found in districts furthest from atmospheric pollution. Large, foliose lichens such as *Lobaria pulmonaria, Lobarina scrobiculata* and *Stictina sylvatica,* are only found in the moist, clean air of western Britain. Compared to such areas as these Shotover has an extremely poor lichen flora. Although a detailed survey has not been completed it is unlikely that there are more than 20 epiphytic species per km[2]. One reason for this is the comparatively dry climate which many lichens cannot tolerate. Coppiced woodland, such as Brasenose and Holly woods is poor for lichens partly because of the dessiccation experienced following underwood removal, and partly because of the shading which several species find intolerable. However, the main reason for Shotover's poor lichen flora is undoubtedly atmospheric pollution originating from Oxford.

The main culprit is thought to be sulphur dioxide (SO_2), a gas produced when both coal and oil are burnt. Lichens are so sensitive to SO_2 pollution that it has proved possible to estimate the level experienced at a site by the presence and abundance of particular epiphytic lichen species [59]. At the highest levels of pollution ($150\mu g\ SO_2/m^3$) no lichens survive and only the alga *Pleurococcus viridis* is found. In Brasenose Wood the presence of *Parmelia saxatilis* and *Hypogymnia physodes,* in addition to the pollution tolerant *Lecanora conizaeoides,* suggests an SO_2 level of about $70\mu g/m^3$. The presence of *Evernia prunastri* in Johnson's Piece suggests that the SO_2 level there may be about $60\mu g/m^3$. The influence of SO_2 on lichen growth is thought to be considerable above $30\mu g/m^3$ and the 'natural' level of SO_2 is $0\text{-}3\mu g/m^3$.

Aspicilia contorta **1**	*C. furcata* **8**	*Parmelia saxatils* **7**
A. calcarea **7**	*C. polydactyla* **1**	*P. caperata* **7**
Bacidia umbrina **1**	*C. pyxidata* **1**	*P. glabratula* **9**
Caloplaca citrina **7**	*C. rangiformis* **1,8**	*P. sulcata* **7-9**
C. decipiens **7**	*C. subulata* **1**	*Physcia caesia* **1-7**
C. heppiana **7**	*Collema tenax* **7**	*P. adsendens* **7**
C. holocarpa **7**	*C. auriculata* **7**	*P. grisea* **1**
C. aurantia **7**	*Dimerella lutea* **1**	*P. orbicularis* **1,7**
C. teichoyta **7**	*Diploicia canescens* **7**	*Physconia grisea* **7**
Candelariella vitellina **1,9**	*Evernaria prunastri* **1,9**	*Ramalina farinacea* **1**
C. aurella **7**	*Hypogymnia physodes* **1,7,8**	*Verrucaria muralis* **7**
C. medians **7**	*Lecanora campestris* **7**	*V. nigrescens* **7**
Cetraria glauca **1**	*L. conizaeoides* **7,9**	*V. viridula* **7**
Cladonia allosquamosa **1**	*L. dispersa* **1,7**	*Xanthoria parietina* **7**
C. chlorophaea **1**	*L. muralis* **1**	*X. aureola* **7**
C. coniocraea **1,8**	*Lecidella stigmatea* **7**	
C. fimbriata **1,8,9**	*Lepraria incana* **7-9**	

Appendix 4

Fungi

Over 260 species of fungi have been recorded from Shotover Forest and many more remain to be identified. Fungi play an extremely important role in the forest ecosystem. The fruiting bodies, most of which appear in autumn, provide food for many animals – from mammals, such as rabbits and squirrels, to beetles (for example the family *Mycetophagidae*), to flies such as the fungus gnats. In addition fungi are important agents of decomposition. Fungal mycelia extract nutrients from dead organic matter and hence play a vital role in mineral recycling.

There is an immense range of shape and colour shown by Shotover's fungi. The large, parasol mushroom is excellent to eat as are ink caps, morels and giant puffball "steaks". However, two extremely poisonous species are also present and a single cap of *Amanita phalloides* or *Lepiota fuscovinacea* is sufficient to cause death to humans even after cooking! The acid grassland on the northern slopes of Shotover Hill has a magnificent range of colourful fungi – green parrot wax caps (*Hygrocybe psittacina*), scarlet wax caps (*H. coccineus*) and vivid yellow wax caps (*H. chlorophanus*).

Several rare fungi have been recorded including woodland species such as *Suillus aeruginescens* and the violet-stemmed *Lepiota bucknallii*, which smells strongly of coal gas, and grassland species such as the green *Leptonia incana* and the blackening wax cap *Hygrocybe nigrescens* which is orange when young, deep red when mature and black in old age.

AGARICALES

Amanita muscaria Fly agaric **1, 8, 9, 13**
A. rubescens The Blusher **1, 8, 9, 13, 16**
A. phalloides Death cap **8, 16**
A. citrina False death cap **1, 8**
A. fulva Tawny grisette **1, 8, 9**
Lepiota procera Parasol mushroom **8, 9, 16**
L. rhacodes Shaggy parasol **1, 2, 8, 12, 16**
L. cristata **8, 9, 16**
L. bucknallii **8, 16**
L. sistrata **8, 16**
L. fuscovinacea **8**
Drosella fracida **8**
Armillaria mellea Honey fungus **1, 7-9, 13, 16**
Oudemansiella radicata Rooting shank **8, 9, 12, 13**
Tricholoma terreum **8**
T. fulvum **8, 9, 13**
T. atrocinereum **8**
Lyophyllum decastes **9**
L. carbonarium **8**
Tricholomopsis rutilans Plums and custard **8, 9, 16**
T. platyphylla **8**
Melanoleuca melaleuca **8**
Leucopaxillus giganteus **8**
Clitocybe geotropa **8**
C. nebularis Clouded agric **7-9, 12**
C. clavipes Club foot **8**
C. infundibuliformis Common funnel cap **7, 8**
C. flaccida Tawny funnel cap **8, 9**
C. fragrans **8**
C. dicolor **9**
Cantharellula cyathiformis The goblet **7, 8**
Laccaria laccata Deceiver **7-9, 12, 16**
L. amethystea Amethyst deceiver **1, 7-9, 12, 14, 16**
Collybia maculata Spotted tough-shank **8, 9, 13, 16**
C. fusipes Spindle shank **12, 16**
C. dryophila **8, 16**
C. confluens Clustered tough-shank **8, 13**

C. erythropus **8**
C. butyracea Butter cap **8, 9, 13**
C. peronata Wood woolly-foot **8, 9, 12, 13**
C. acervata **8**
Flammulina velutipes Velvet shank **1, 7-9**
Hygrophorus cossus Goat moth wax cap **8**
H. leucophaeus **8**
H. lucorum Larch wax cap **8**
H. citrinus **8**
Hygrocybe pratensis Meadow wax cap **1**
H. coccineus Scarlet wax cap **1**
H. nigrescens Blackening wax cap **1, 8**
H. conicus Conical wax cap **8**
H. chlorophanus Yellow wax cap **1**
H. nivea Snowy wax cap **1**
H. psittacina Parrot wax cap **1, 8**
Hygrophoropsis aurantiaca False chantarelle **8, 9, 16**
Marasmius androsaceus Horse-hair fungus **8**
M. ramealis **7, 8, 12**
M. rotula **8, 9, 12, 16**

Blackening wax cap (Hygrocybe nigrescens)

Fungi

Fungi

Morel (Morchella esculenta)

Appendix 5

Vascular Plants

631 species of vascular plant have been recorded from Shotover over the past two centuries – a very substantial number when you consider that the total list for the British Isles is about 2400. Of the 631 species 97 are now thought to be extinct, which represents 15.4% of the total. This loss of 15.4% of the vascular plants over 200 years is a dramatic indication of the habitat changes which have taken place. It will be most interesting to review the situation in a further 200 years.

Of the plants remaining at Shotover one national rarity remains which has been omitted from all lists for security reasons. Several locally uncommon species are to be found including columbine (*Aquilegia vulgaris*), wild service tree (*Sorbus torminalis*), meadow saffron (*Colchicum autumnale*), herb-Paris (*Paris quadrifolia*), wild daffodil (*Narcissus pseudonarcissus*) and green-flowered helleborine (*Epipactis phyllanthes*).

LYCOPODIACEAE
* *Huperzia selago*   Fir clubmoss   **1** (1822 Baxter)
* *Lycopodium clavatum*
   Stag's horn clubmoss   **1** (1866 Baxter)
EQUISETACEAE
   Equisetum palustre   Marsh horsetail   **8,9,13**
* *E. sylvaticum*   Wood horsetail   **1** (Baxter)
   E. arvense   Common horsetail   **1,8,9,12,13**
   E. telmateia   Giant horsetail   **2,4,8,9,11-13**
OPHIOGLOSSACEAE
   Ophioglossum vulgatum   Adder's-tongue fern   **1,8,13**
* *Botrychium lunaria*   Moonwort   **1** (1844 Druce)
HYPOLEPIDACEAE
   Pteridium aquilinum   Bracken   **1,4,7-9,13,14**
THELYPTERIDACEAE
* *Thelypteris limbosperma*   Mountain fern   **1** (1858 Boswell)
ASPLENIACEAE
   Phyllitis scolopendrium   Hart's-tongue fern   **1,8,13**
ATHYRIACEAE
   Athyrium filix-femina   Lady fern   **9**

ASPIDIACEAE
* *Polystichum aculeatum*   Hard shield-fern   **1** (1884 Boswell)
   P. setiferum   Soft shield-fern   **9**
   Dryopteris filix-mas   Male fern   **1,7-9,11-13,16**
   D. borreri   Scaly male fern   **7**
* *D. cristata*   Crested buckler-fern   **1** (c. 1890)
   D. carthusiana   Narrow buckler-fern   **7**
   D. dilatata   Broad buckler-fern   **1,7-9,12-14**
BLECHNACEAE
* *Blechnum spicant*   Hard fern   **1** (1885)
PINACEAE
   Abies grandis   Giant fir   **8**
   Picea abies   Norway spruce   **8,12-14**
   Tsuga heterophylla   Western hemlock   **8**
   Larix decidua   European larch   **8,13-15**
   Pinus sylvestris   Scots pine   **1,8,13-16**
   P. nigra   Austrian pine   **1**
   P. nigra ssp. laricio   Corsican pine   **8**
CUPRESSACEAE
   Chamaecyparis lawsoniana   Lawson's cypress   **8,14**

  Adder's-tongue fern (Ophioglossum vulgatum)

Vascular Plants

TAXACEAE
Taxus baccata   Yew   **7-10,13**
SALICACEAE
Salix fragilis   Crack willow   **1,2,7-9,13**
S. alba   White wilow   **1,11**
S. cinerea   Grey willow   **8,9,12,13,15**
S. caprea   Goat willow   **2,4,7-9,11-13,15,17**
S. viminalis   Common osier   **7,8**
Populus canescens   Grey poplar   **1**
P. tremula   Aspen   **1,7,8,12,15**
P. gileadensis   Balsam poplar   **8**
P. x canadensis   Italian poplar   **2**
BETULACEAE
Betula pendula   Silver birch   **1,7-16**
B. pubescens   Downy birch   **1,7**
Alnus glutinosa   Alder   **13**
CORYLACEAE
Carpinus betulus   Hornbeam   **8,9,11**
Corylus avellana   Hazel   **4,7-17**
FAGACEAE
Fagus sylvatica   Beech   **1,4,7-9,11,13,14**
Castanea sativa   Sweet chestnut   **1,8**
Quercus cerris   Turkey oak   **1,10**
Q. petraea   Sessile oak   **2,8**
Q. robur   Pedunculate oak   **1-17**
ULMACEAE
Ulmus glabra   Wych elm   **7-9,11,13**
U. procera   English elm   **4,7,9,11-14**
CANNABACEAE
Humulus lupulus   Hop   **1,7,8,16**
URTICACEAE
Urtica dioica   Common nettle   **1-17**
U. urens   Small nettle   near **8**
POLYGONACEAE
Polygonum aviculare   Knotgrass   **4,7,8,16**
P. hydropiper   Water-pepper   **1,7**
P. persicaria   Redshank   **4,7,8**
P. lapathifolium   Pale persicaria   **13**
Bilderdykia convolvulus   Black-bindweed   **2,8**
Rumex acetosella   Sheep's sorrel   **1,8,9,12**
R. acetosa   Common sorrel   **3,4,6,8,9**
R. crispus   Curled dock   **7,8**
R. conglomeratus   Clustered dock   **4,13**
R. sanguineus   Wood dock   **7-9,11,13,15**
R. obtusifolius   Broad-leaved dock   **4,7-9,13,15,17**
CHENOPODIACEAE
Chenopodium polyspermum
   Many-seeded goosefoot   near **8**
C. album   Fat-hen   **7,8**
Atriplex patula   Common orache   **8**
A. hastata   Hastate orache   **8**
PORTULACACEAE
* *Montia fontana*   Blinks   **1** (1790 Sibthorp)
CARYOPHYLLACEAE
Arenaria serpyllifolia   Thyme-leaved sandwort   **1,8**
A. leptoclados   Slender sandwort   **1**
Moehringia trinervia
   Three-veined sandwort   **7-9,11,13-15**
* *Minuartia hybrida*   Fine-leaved sandwort   **1** (1896)
Stellaria media   Common chickweed   **1,4,6-9,14,15**
S. pallida   Lesser chickweed   **8**
S. holostea   Greater stitchwort   **1,7,9,11-14**

S. alsine   Bog stitchwort   **1,9**
S. graminea   Lesser stitchwort   **1,4,8,11,15**
Cerastium arvense   Field mouse-ear   **8**
C. fontanum   Common mouse-ear   **1,2,4,8**
C. glomeratum   Sticky mouse-ear   **1,3,8**
C. semidecandrum   Little mouse-ear   **1**
* *Sagina nodosa*   Knotted pearlwort   **1** (Sibthorp)
S. procumbens   Procumbent pearlwort   **1,8,9**
Scleranthus annuus   Annual knawel   **1**
Spergula arvensis   Corn spurrey   **1,8,9**
Spergularia rubra   Sand spurrey   **1**
Lychnis flos-cuculi   Ragged-robin   **1,5,7,8,11,12,15**
* *Argrostemma githago*
   Corncockle   **1,8,16** (c. 1830 Boswell)
Silene vulgaris   Bladder campion   **7,8,16**
* *S. noctiflora*   Night-flowering catchfly   **1,8** (1928)
S. alba   White campion   **1,7,8**
S. dioica   Red campion   **1,4,7,8,11**
* *S. gallica*   Small-flowered catchfly   **8** (1886)
CERATOPHYLLACEAE
Ceratophyllum demersum   Rigid hornwort   **8**
RANUNCULACEAE
Caltha palustris   Marsh-marigold   **1,5,7-9,13**
Anemone nemorosa   Wood anemone   **7,8,11-17**
Clematis vitalba   Traveller's-joy   **7,8,11,12,16**
Ranunculus repens
   Creeping buttercup   **1,3,4,7-9,11,12,17**
R. acris   Meadow buttercup   **1,3,4,8-10**
R. bulbosus   Bulbous buttercup   **1,8**
* *R. arvensis*   Corn buttercup   **8** (1886)
* *R. parviflorus*   Small-flowered buttercup   **1** (1886)
R. auricomus   Goldilocks   **7,8,12,14,15,17**
R. sceleratus   Celery-leaved buttercup   **8**
R. ficaria   Lesser celandine   **1,7-9,11-17**
R. flammula   Lesser spearwort   **1,4,7**
R. aquatilis   Water-crowfoot   **9,13**
Myosurus minimus   Mousetail   **8**
Aquilegia vulgaris   Columbine   **8**
Thalictrum flavum   Common meadow-rue   **2**
PAPAVERACEAE
Papaver rhoeas   Common poppy   **1,8,9**
P. dubium   Long-headed poppy   **8**
P. argemone   Prickly poppy   **8**
* *P. hybridum*   Rough poppy   **1** (1860 H. Boswell)
Chelidonium majus   Greater celandine   **1**
Fumaria officinalis   Common fumitory   **1,8**
CRUCIFERAE
Sisymbrium officinale   Hedge mustard   **2,8**
Alliaria petiolata   Garlic mustard   **7-9,14,17**
Arabidopsis thaliana   Thale cress   **8**
Barbarea vulgaris   Winter-cress   **7,8**
Nasturtium officinale   Water-cress   **1,7,13**
Cardamine amara   Large bitter-cress   **8**
C. pratensis   Cuckoo flower   **7-9,13-15**
C. flexuosa   Wavy bitter-cress   **7,8,14**
C. hirsuta   Hairy bitter-cress   **8,14,17**
* *Arabis hirsuta*   Hairy rock-cress   **1** (1831)
Lunaria annua   Honesty   **1**
Erophila verna   Common whitlow-grass   **8**
Capsella bursa-pastoris   Shepherd's purse   **2,5,8,9**
Thlaspi arvense   Field penny-cress   **7,8**
* *Lepidium campestre*   Field pepperwort   **1** (W. Baxter)

* *Coronopus squamatus*   Swine-cress   **1** (19c Druce)
Brassica napus   Rape   **8**
B. rapa   Wild turnip   **2,8**
Sinapis arvensis   Charlock   **2,7,8**
Raphanus raphanistrum   Wild radish   **8**
RESEDACEAE
Reseda luteola   Weld   **1,6,8,16**
R. lutea   Wild mignonette   **1,6,8**
DROSERACEAE
* *Drosera rotundifolia*   Round-leaved sundew   **1** (Sibthorp)
CRASSULACEAE
Sedum telephium   Orpine   **7**
S. acre   Biting stonecrop   **2**
S. album   White stonecrop   **2**
* *S. dasyphyllum*   Thick-leaved stonecrop   **1** (1886)
SAXIFRAGACEAE
* *Saxifraga granulata*
   Meadow saxifrage   **8,16** (1927 Druce)
Chrysosplenium oppositifolium
   Opposite-leaved golden saxifrage   **7-9,11**
PARNASSIACEAE
* *Parnassia palustris*   Grass-of-Parnassus   **1,8,11** (1896)
GROSSULARIACEAE
Ribes rubrum   Red currant   **7-9,12,13,16**
R. nigrum   Black currant   **7,13**
R. sanguineum   Flowering currant   **1**
R. uva-crispa   Gooseberry   **7,8,12,14,16**
ROSACEAE
Filipendula vulgaris   Dropwort   **6,8**
F. ulmaria   Meadowsweet   **1,4,5,11,12,14,15,17**
Rubus idaeus   Raspberry   **2,7,13,16**
R. fruticosus agg.   Blackberry   **1-17**
R. caesius   Dewberry   **2,8,14**
Rosa arvensis   Field rose   **7,8,12**
R. canina   Dog rose   **1,2,4,7,8,13-17**
R. rubiginosa   Sweet briar   **8**
Agrimonia eupatoria   Agrimony   **1,2,4,8,15,16**
A. procera   Fragrant agrimony   **2,8**
Sanguisorba officinalis   Great burnet   **3,5**

S. minor   Salad burnet   **6,8**
Geum rivale   Water avens   **8,11,12,17**
G. urbanum   Wood avens   **1,7-9,11-17**
Potentilla anserina   Silverweed   **3,4,7-9,14**
P. erecta   Tormentil   **1,7,8,15**
P. reptans   Creeping cinquefoil   **2,6-8,14-16**
P. sterilis   Barren strawberry   **7,8,11,12,14-17**
Fragaria vesca   Wild strawberry   **7,8,12-14**
* *Alchemilla vulgaris* agg.   Lady's mantle   **16** (Sibthorp)
Aphanes arvensis   Parsley piert   **1,8,9**
A. microcarpa   **1,9**
* *Pyrus pyraster*   Pear   **1** (1858 H. Boswell)
Malus sylvestris   Crab apple   **1,7-9,11,12,15,16**
Sorbus aucuparia   Rowan   **1,7,8,16**
S. torminalis   Wild service tree   **1,14,15**
S. aria   Common white beam   **1**
S. intermedia   **8**
Crataegus laevigata   Midland hawthorn   **7,11,12,15**
C. monogyna   Hawthorn   **1-17**
Prunus spinosa   Blackthorn   **1,2,6-8,10-17**
P. domestica   Wild plum   **1,7,8**
P. avium   Wild cherry   **1,7-9,11-14,16**
P. padus   Bird cherry   **1**
P. laurocerasus   Cherry laurel   **7**
LEGUMINOSAE
* *Cytisus scoparius*   Broom   **1** (S. Laing)
Ulex europaeus   Gorse   **1,4,6-9,13,16**
Galega officinalis   Goat's rue   **2**
Astralagus glycyphyllos   Wild liquorice   **8**
Vicia cracca   Tufted vetch   **1,2,7,8,13,15**
V. hirsuta   Hairy tare   **2,8**
V. tetrasperma   Smooth tare   **2,8**
V. sepium   Bush vetch   **7-17**
V. sativa   Common vetch   **1,2,8,9**
* *V. lathyroides*   Spring vetch   **16** (H. Boswell)
* *Lathyrus montanus*   Bitter vetch   **1** (1886 R.C. Pryor)
L. pratensis   Meadow vetchling   **2,3,8,13,15**
L. tuberosus   Tuberous pea   **2**
L. sylvestris   Narrow-leaved everlasting pea   **7**
L. nissolia   Grass vetchling   **2**
Ononis repens   Common restharrow   **1,8**
Melilotus officinalis   Ribbed melilot   **1**
Medicago lupulina   Black medick   **1,6,8,13**
M. sativa   Lucerne   **1,8**
Trifolium repens   White clover   **1-4,7-9,13,15**
T. hybridum   Alsike clover   **2**
* *T. fragiferum*   Strawberry clover   **8**
T. campestre   Hop trefoil   **2,8**
T. micranthum   Slender trefoil   **7**
T. striatum   Knotted trefoil   **1**
* *T. arvense*   Hare's-foot clover   **8** (1884)
* *T. scabrum*   Rough trefoil   **1** (1823)
T. pratense   Red clover   **1-4,6-9**
T. medium   Zigzag clover   **1,2**
* *T. subterraneum*   Subterranean trefoil   **1** (1830 Baxter)
Lotus corniculatus   Common bird's-foot trefoil   **1-3,6-8**
L. uliginosus   Greater bird's-foot trefoil   **1,2,4,7,8,15**
Anthyllis vulneraria   Kidney vetch   **6,8**
Ornithopus perpusillus   Bird's-foot   **1**
Hippocrepis comosa   Horseshoe vetch   **6**
OXALIDACEAE
Oxalis acetosella   Wood sorrel   **7-10,12,13**

   Opposite-leaved golden saxifrage (Chrysosplenium oppositifolium)

Vascular Plants

GERANIACEAE
Geranium pyrenaicum   Hedgerow cranes-bill   **1**
G. molle   Dove's-foot cranes-bill   **2,7,8**
G. pusillum   Small-flowered cranes-bill   **8**
G. columbinum   Long-stalked cranes-bill   **8**
* *G. lucidum*   Shining cranes-bill   **5**
G. dissectum   Cut-leaved cranes-bill   **2,8**
G. robertianum   Herb-Robert   **7-9,11-17**
Erodium cicutarium   Common stork's-bill   **8**
LINACEAE
Linum cartharticum   Fairy flax   **6,8**
EUPHORBIACEAE
Mercurialis perennis   Dog's mecury   **7-17**
Euphorbia helioscopia   Sun spurge   **2,8**
E. lathyris   Caper spurge   **8**
E. exigua   Dwarf spurge   **8**
E. peplus   Petty spurge   **2**
E. amygdaloides   Wood spurge   **7,8,10-14,16,17**
POLYGALACEAE
Polygala vulgaris   Common milkwort   **1,8**
ACERACEAE
Acer platanoides   Norway maple   **1,8**
A. campestre   Field maple   **1,7,8,11,12,14-16**
A. pseudoplatanus   Sycamore   **1,4,6-9,11-16**
A. saccharum   Sugar maple   **1**
HIPPOCASTANACEAE
Aesculus hippocastanum   Horse chestnut   **1,2,8,9,11**
BALSAMINACEAE
Impatiens parviflora   Small balsam   **1,4**
I. glandulifera   Indian balsam   **1**
AQUIFOLIACEAE
Ilex aquifolium   Holly   **1,7-9,11,14-17**
CELASTRACEAE
Eunoymus europaeus   Spindle   **7,8,11,12,14**
STAPHYLEACEAE
Staphylea pinnata   Bladder-nut   **8**
BUXACEAE
Buxus sempervirens   Box   **8,9**
RHAMNACEAE
Rhamnus catharticus   Buckthorn   **7,8**
TILIACEAE
Tilia x vulgaris   Lime   **8,13**
MALVACEAE
Malva moschata   Musk mallow   **1,8**
M. sylvestris   Common mallow   **1,8**
M. neglecta   Dwarf mallow   **2,8**
THYMELAEACEAE
* *Daphne mezereum*   Mezereon   **1** (1832 R.C. Pryor)
D. laureola   Spurge laurel   **7,9,11**
GUTTIFERAE
* *Hypericum androseanum*   Tutsan   **1** (1831 Baxter)
H. hirsutum   Hairy St. John's-wort   **7,8,11-14,17**
H. pulchrum   Slender St. John's-wort   **7,8**
* *H. elodes*   Marsh St. John's-wort   **8** (1857)
H. humifusum   Trailing St. John's-wort   **8**
H. tetrapterum   Square-stalked St. John's-wort   **8,11,13**
* *H. maculatum*   Imperforate St. John's-wort   **8** (1974)
H. perforatum   Perforate St. John's-wort   **6-9,14-16**
VIOLACEAE
Viola odorata   Sweet violet   **1,8,12,16**
V. hirta   Hairy violet   **2,6,8**
V. reichenbachiana   Early dog-violet   **7-9,11,12,17**

V. riviniana   Common dog-violet   **7-9,11-15**
* *V. palustris*   Marsh violet   **16**
V. arvensis   Field pansy   **8,9**
CISTACEAE
Helianthemum nummularium
   Common rock-rose   **6,8,16**
CUCURBITACEAE
Bryonia cretica   White bryony   **6-8**
LYTHRACEAE
Lythrum salicaria   Purple-loosestrife   **8**
* *L. portula*   Water-purslane   **13** (W. Baxter)
ONAGRACEAE
Circaea lutetiana
   Enchanter's-nightshade   **7-9,11-13,15**
Epilobium angustifolium
   Rose bay willowherb   **7-9,11-13, 15**
E. hirsutum   Great willowherb   **4,7-9,11,15,17**
E. parviflorum   Hoary willowherb   **4,7,8**
E. montanum   Broad-leaved willowherb   **7,8,11,14,15**
* *E. palustre*   Marsh willowherb   **8** (1886)
E. adenocaulon   American willowherb   **7,8**
CORNACEAE
Cornus sanguinea   Dogwood   **7,8,11,12,14-17**
ARALIACEAE
Hedera helix   Ivy   **1,2,7-17**
UMBELLIFERAE
Hydrocotyle vulgaris   Marsh pennywort   **8**
Sanicula europaea   Sanicle   **7,8,12**
Anthriscus sylvestris   Cow parsley   **1-17**
* *A. caucalis*   Bur chervil   **1** (1859 H. Boswell)
Conopodium majus   Pignut   **1,7,8,11-13,16**
Pimpinella major   Greater burnet-saxifrage   **1,7,8**
P. saxifraga   Burnet-saxifrage   **3,5,6,8,16**
Aegopodium podagraria   Ground-elder   **8,13**

Early dog-violet (Viola reichenbachiana)

Vascular Plants

Oenanthe fistulosa   Tubular water-dropwort   **1**
O. lachenalii   Parsley water-dropwort   **8**
Aethusa cynapium   Fool's parsley   **8**
Silaum silaus   Pepper-saxifrage   **8**
Conium maculatum   Hemlock   **8,11**
* *Bupleurum rotundifolium*   Thorow-wax   **2** (H. Boswell)
Apium nodiflorum   Fool's water-cress   **4,7-9,11,17**
* *Petroselinum segetum*   Corn parsley   **1** (1884)
* *Sison amomum*   Stone parsley   **1** (Sibthorp)
* *Carum carvi*   Caraway   **8** (1974)
Angelica sylvestris   Wild angelica   **1,4,5,7-9,11-14**
Pastinaca sativa   Wild parsnip   **16**
Heracleum sphondylium   Hogweed   **1-17**
* *Torilis nodosa*   Knotted hedge-parsley   **1** (H. Boswell)
* *T. arvensis*   Spreading hedge-parsley   **1** (H. Boswell)
T. japonica   Upright hedge-parsley   **1,7,15**
Daucus carota   Wild carrot   **1,2,6,8**
ERICACEAE
Calluna vulgaris   Heather   **1,8**
PRIMULACEAE
Primula vulgaris   Primrose   **7,8,11-17**
P. veris   Cowslip   **7,8**
P. veris x vulgaris   False oxlip   **8**
Lysimachia nemorum   Yellow pimpernel   **1,4,8,11,13**
L. vulgaris   Yellow loosestrife   **8**
L. nummularia   Creeping jenny   **1,7-9,11,14,15**
Anagallis tenella   Bog pimpernel   **8**
A. arvensis   Scarlet pimpernel   **1,8**
Samolus valerandi   Brookweed   **8**
OLEACEAE
Fraxinus excelsior   Ash   **1,2,4,6-16**
Syringa vulgaris   Lilac   **2**
Ligustrum vulgare   Wild privet   **7,8,11,12,14-17**
GENTIANACEAE
Centaurium erythraea   Common centaury   **1,8**
* *Gentianella campestris*   Field gentian   **1** (1819 Dillenius)
* *G. amarella*   Autumn gentian   **1,8** (1886)
MENYANTHACEAE
* *Menyanthes trifoliata*   Bogbean   **1,8,16** (1886)
APOCYNACEAE
Vinca minor   Lesser periwinkle   **14**
RUBIACEAE
Sherardia arvensis   Field madder   **8**
* *Asperula cyanchica*   Squinancy wort   **6** (1886)
Galium odoratum   Woodruff   **7,12**
G. uliginosum   Fen bedstraw   **8**
G. palustre   Common marsh-bedstraw   **7,9**
G. verum   Lady's bedstraw   **1,4,6,8,16**
G. x pomeranicum   **8**
G. mollugo   Hedge bedstraw   **1,7,8,17**
G. saxatile   Heath bedstraw   **1**
G. aparine   Cleavers   **1,6,8,9,11-14,17**
* *Cruciata laevipes*   Crosswort   **8** (1886)
CONVOLVULACEAE
* *Cuscuta epithymum*   Dodder   **1** (H.E. Garnsey)
Calystegia sepium   Hedge bindweed   **6,13**
Convolvulus arvensis   Field bindweed   **1,8**
BORAGINACEAE
* *Lithospermum officinale*
   Common gromwell   **8,16** (1886)
Echium vulgare   Viper's-bugloss   **8,16**
Anchusa arvensis   Bugloss   **8**

Myosotis arvensis   Field forget-me-not   **1,8,9,11,12,16**
M. ramosissima   Early forget-me-not   **8**
M. discolor   Changing forget-me-not   **1,8**
M. laxa   Tufted forget-me-not   **1**
VERBENACEAE
Verbena officinalis   Vervain   **6**
CALLITRICHACEAE
Callitriche stagnalis   Common water-starwort   **7,13-15**
LABIATAE
Ajuga reptans   Bugle   **1,7-9,11-17**
* *Teucrium scorodonia*   Wood sage   **1** (1860 W. Holladay)
Galeopsis tetrahit   Common hemp-nettle   **7,8**
Lamium maculatum   Spotted dead-nettle   **10**
L. album   White dead-nettle   **1,2,7-9,14,16**
L. purpureum   Read dead-nettle   **1,7,8**
L. hybridum   Cut-leaved dead-nettle   **8**
L. amplexicaule   Henbit dead-nettle   **8**
Lamiastrum galeobdolon
   Yellow archangel   **1,7,8,11-13,17**
Ballota nigra   Black horehound   **1,2,8,16**
Stachys officinalis   Betony   **7,11,14,15**
S. sylvatica   Hedge woundwort   **1,2,4,7-9,11-14**
* *S. arvensis*   Field woundwort   **8** (1974)
Glechoma hederacea   Ground-ivy   **1,2,4,6-17**
Prunella vulgaris   Selfheal   **1,2,4,7,8,11-14**
Melissa officinalis   Balm   **10**
Acinos arvensis   Basil thyme   **8**
Clinopodium vulgare   Wild basil   **2,7,8,16**
Thymus praecox   Wild thyme   **6,8**
T. pulegioides   Large thyme   **8**
Lycopus europaeus   Gipsywort   **1,8**
Mentha arvensis   Corn mint   **8**
M. aquatica   Water mint   **1,3,4,7-9**
M. spicata   Spear mint   **7**
SOLANACEAE
Atropa bella-donna
   Deadly nightshade   **7** (2 plants 1980)
Hyoscyamus niger   Henbane   **7** (1976-77), **8** (1980)
Solanum nigrum   Black nightshade   **8,13**
S. dulcamara   Bittersweet   **1,4,7-9,11-17**
SCROPHULARIACEAE
Verbascum thapsus   Great mullein   **7,8**
* *Scrophularia nodosa*   Common figwort   **1, 7-9, 11-15**
S. auriculata   Water figwort   **1, 3, 7-9, 11-14, 17**
* *Misopates orontium*   Lesser snapdragon   **1**
Chaenorhinum minus   Small toadflax   **8**
Linaria vulgaris   Common toadflax   **8**
Kickxia elatine   Sharp-leaved fluellen   **8**
Digitalis purpurea   Foxglove   **1, 7, 8**
Veronica serpyllifolia
   Thyme-leaved speedwell   **1,7-9,14**
V. officinalis   Heath speedwell   **1, 8**
V. chamaedrys
   Germander speedwell   **1,2,7-9,11,12,14**
V. montana   Wood speedwell   **7, 9, 11**
V. beccabunga   Brooklime   **1, 4, 5, 7-9, 12, 14, 15, 17**
V. arvensis   Wall speedwell   **1, 8, 9**
V. polita   Grey field-speedwell   **1**
V. persica   Common field-speedwell   **2, 8, 9**
V. hederifolia   Ivy-leaved speedwell   **8, 13**
Melampyrum pratense   Common cow-wheat   **7**
Euphrasia nemorosa   Common eyebright   **8**

Vascular Plants

Odontites verna   Red bartsia   **1-3, 8, 16**
* *Pedicularis palustris*   Marsh lousewort   **1, 8, 16** (1886)
P. sylvatica   Lousewort   **1**
Rhinanthus minor   Yellow rattle   **5, 8**
Lathraea squamaria   Toothwort   **8**
OROBANCHACEAE
Orobanche minor   Common broomrape   **2, 8**
LENTIBULARIACEAE
* *Pinguicula vulgaris*   Common butterwort   **8** (1885)
PLANTAGINACEAE
Plantago major   Greater plantain   **1-4, 7-9, 13, 15, 16**
* *P. coronopus*   Buck's-horn plantain   **1** (1823 Baxter)
P. media   Hoary plantain   **1, 7, 8**
P. lanceolata   Ribwort plantain   **1-3, 6-9**
CAPRIFOLIACEAE
Sambucus nigra   Elder   **1-17**
Viburnum opulus   Guelder-rose   **1, 4, 7, 8, 12, 14, 15**
V. lantana   Wayfaring-tree   **7, 8, 12, 15, 17**
Symphoricarpos albus   Snowberry   **1, 5, 9, 11**
Lonicera periclymenum   Honeysuckle   **1-17**
ADOXACEAE
Adoxa moschatellina   Moschatel   **1, 7-9, 12-14, 16**
VALERIANACEAE
Valerianella locusta   Common cornsalad   **6**
Valeriana officinalis   Common valerian   **1, 8, 9, 11, 15**
V. dioica   Marsh valerian   **8**
DIPSACACEAE
Dipsacus fullonum   Teasel   **2, 7, 14, 17**
Succisa pratensis   Devil's-bit scabious   **3, 7, 8**
Knautia arvensis   Field scabious   **2, 6, 8**
Scabiosa columbaria   Small scabious   **2**
CAMPANULACEAE
Campanula glomerata   Clustered bellflower   **6**
* *C. latifolia*   Greater bellflower   **1** (1890)
C. trachelium   Nettle-leaved bellflower   **7, 8, 12**
C. rapunculoides   Creeping bellflower   **2**
C. rotundifolia   Harebell   **1, 4, 8**
Legousia hybrida   Venus's looking-glass   **8**
* *Jasione montana*   Sheep's-bit   **1** (1886)
COMPOSITAE
Eupatorium cannabinum   Hemp-agrimony   **2, 8**
Solidago canadensis   Canadian goldenrod   **2, 7**
Bellis perennis   Daisy   **1-17**
Aster novi-belgii   Michaelmas daisy   **2**
Erigeron acer   Blue fleabane   **6, 8**
Conyza canadensis   Canadian fleabane   **8**
* *Filago pyramidata*
   Broad-leaved cudweed   **1** (1927 Druce)
* *Logfia minima*   Small cudweed   **1**
Omalotheca sylvatica   Heath cudweed   **8**
Filaginella uliginosa   Marsh cudweed   **7, 8**
Inula conyza   Ploughman's-spikenard   **8**
Pulicaria dysenterica   Common fleabane   **1-4, 8**
* *Bidens cernua*   Nodding bur-marigold   **1** (Sibthorp)
Anthemis arvensis   Corn chamomile   **8**
Achillea ptarmica   Sneezewort   **5**
A. millefolium   Yarrow   **1-17**
Matricaria perforata   Scentless mayweed   **1, 8**
Chamomilla suaveolens   Pineappleweed   **1, 8**
Chrysanthemum segetum   Corn marigold   **1, 8**
Tanacetum vulgare   Tansy   **1, 8**
Leucanthemum vulgare   Oxeye daisy   **1, 2, 8**

Artemisia vulgaris   Mugwort   **1, 6-8, 16**
Tussilago farfara   Coltsfoot   **1, 7-9, 11, 13, 17**
* *Senecio fluviatilis*   Broad-leaved ragwort   **1** (1886)
S. jacobaea   Common ragwort   **1-17**
S. erucifolius   Hoary ragwort   **2, 8**
S. squalidus   Oxford ragwort   **8**
* *S. sylvaticus*   Heath groundsel   **8** (1974)
S. viscosus   Sticky groundsel   **8**
S. vulgaris   Groundsel   **2, 7, 8, 11**
Carlina vulgaris   Carline thistle   **8**
Arctium minus   Lesser burdock   **1, 7-9, 11, 12, 14, 17**
Carduus nutans   Musk thistle   **1, 7, 8**
C. crispus   Welted thistle   **8**
Cirsium eriophorum   Woolly thistle   **2, 8**
C. vulgare   Spear thistle   **2, 4, 8, 9, 11-13, 15**
C. acaule   Dwarf thistle   **8**
C. palustre   Marsh thistle   **4, 7-9, 11, 12, 14, 15**
C. arvense   Creeping thistle   **1-17**
* *Onopordum acanthium*   Cotton thistle   **1** (1884)
Serratula tinctoria   Saw-wort   **7**
Centaurea scabiosa   Greater knapweed   **2, 6, 8, 16**
* *C. solstitialis*   Yellow star-thistle   **1** (1886)
C. nigra   Common knapweed   **2, 3, 8**
C. cyanus   Cornflower   **8** (1981)
* *Cichorium intybus*   Chicory   **8** (1974)
Hypochoeris radicata   Cat's-ear   **8, 9**

Vascular Plants

Leontodon autumnalis   Autumn hawkbit   **1, 8**
L. hispidus   Rough hawkbit   **7, 8**
L. taraxacoides   Lesser hawkbit   **1, 8**
Picris echioides   Bristly oxtongue   **2, 8, 15**
Tragapogon pratensis   Goat's-beard   **2**
Sonchus asper   Prickly sow-thistle   **2, 8**
S. oleraceus   Smooth sow-thistle   **2, 8, 13**
S. arvensis   Perennial sow-thistle   **2, 8**
Lactuca serriola   Prickly lettuce   **7**
Mycelis muralis   Wall lettuce   **8**
Taraxacum officinale   Dandelion   **1-17**
Lapsana communis   Nipplewort   **1, 7, 8, 15**
Crepis biennis   Rough hawk's-beard   **7, 8**
C. capillaris   Smooth hawk's-beard   **8, 15**
C. vesicaria   Beaked hawk's-beard   **7**
Hieracium pilosella   Mouse-ear hawkweed   **8**
H. murorum agg.   Few-leaved hawkweed   **8**
H. umbellatum agg.   Leafy hawkweed   **1, 7**
HYDROCHARITACEAE
Elodea canadensis   Canadian pondweed   **9**
JUNGAGINACEAE
* *Triglochin palustris*   Marsh arrowgrass   **8** (1926 Druce)
POTAMOGETONACEAE
Potamogeton natans   Broad-leaved pondweed   **13**
P. compressus   Grass-wrack pondweed   **9**
P. pectinatus   Fennel pondweed   **13**
LILIACEAE
Colchicum autumnale   Meadow saffron   **12**
* *Gagea lutea*   Yellow star-of-Bethlehem   **16** (1926)
Ornithogalum umbellatum   Star-of-Bethlehem   **1**
Hyacinthoides non-scripta   Bluebell   **1, 7-9, 11-17**
Allium ursinum   Ramsons   **8, 11, 12, 14-16**
A. vineale   Crow garlic   **2, 8**
Convallaria majalis   Lily-of-the-Valley   near **8**
Paris quadrifolia   Herb-Paris   **8, 12**
Ruscus aculeatus   Butcher's-broom   **2**
AMARYLLIDACEAE
Galanthus nivalis   Snowdrop   **7**
Narcissus pseudonarcissus   Wild daffodil   **11, 12**
N. hispanicus   Daffodil   **7, 12**
DIOSCOREACEAE
Tamus communis   Black bryony   **7, 8, 11, 12, 15, 16**
IRIDACEAE
Iris foetidissima   Stinking iris   near **8, 12, 13**
I. pseudacorus   Yellow iris   **8, 12**
JUNCACEAE
Juncus inflexus   Hard rush   **1, 4, 7-9, 13, 15, 17**
J. effusus   Soft rush   **1, 4, 7-9, 11, 13-17**
J. conglomeratus   Compact rush   **8, 15**
J. bufonius   Toad rush   **7, 8, 15**
J. subnodulosus   Blunt-flowered rush   **8**
J. acutiflorus   Sharp-flowered rush   **3, 7, 8**
J. articulatus   Jointed rush   **1, 8, 15**
Luzula campestris   Field woodrush   **1, 8, 9**
L. multiflora   Heath woodrush   **7**
* *L. sylvatica*   Greater woodrush   **8** (1974)
L. pilosa   Hairy woodrush   **7, 8, 14, 15**
GRAMINEAE
Festuca gigantea   Giant fescue   **7, 8, 11-15**
F. pratensis   Meadow fescue   **1, 2, 8**
F. arundinacea   Tail fescue   **2, 8**
F. rubra   Red fescue   **1, 2, 4, 8**

F. ovina   Sheep's-fescue   **1, 8**
x *Festulolium loliaceum*   **7**
Lolium perenne   Perennial rye-grass   **1-16**
L. multiflorum   Italian rye-grass   **8**
Vulpia bromoides   Squirreltail fescue   **1**
* *V. myuros*   Rat's-tail fescue   **1** (1886)
* *Desmazeria rigida*   Hard poa   **1** (1886)
Poa annua   Annual meadow-grass   **1-17**
P. trivialis   Rough meadow-grass   **1-5, 7-9, 12, 13, 15**
P. pratensis   Smooth meadow-grass   **1, 2, 4, 7, 8**
P. nemoralis   Wood meadow-grass   **7, 8, 11, 12, 14, 15**
Dactylis glomerata   Cock's-foot   **1-3, 5, 6, 8, 9, 11-14**
Cynosurus cristatus   Crested dog's-tail   **2, 3, 6, 8, 11, 15**
Briza media   Quaking-grass   **6, 8**
Melica uniflora   Wood melick   **7-9**
Glyceria fluitans   Floating sweet-grass   **7, 15**
G. plicata   Plicate sweet-grass   **8**
Bromus sterilis   Barren brome   **1, 6, 8, 9**
B. ramosus   Hairy-brome   **7, 8, 10, 11**
B. erectus   Upright brome   **6, 8**
B. commutatus   Meadow brome   **2**
B. hordeaceus   Soft-brome   **1, 2**
Brachypodium sylvaticum
   False-brome   **1, 7-9, 11, 12, 14, 15**
B. pinnatum   Tor-grass   **8**
Elymus caninus   Bearded couch   **7, 8, 15**
E. repens   Common couch   **1, 7, 8**
Hordeum murinum   Wall barley   **1, 2, 5, 7**
* *H. secalinum*   Meadow barley   **8** (1974)
Avena fatua   Wild-oat   **1**
Avenula pubescens   Downy oat-grass   **8**
A. pratensis   Meadow oat-grass   **3, 8**
Arrhenatherum elatius
   False oat-grass   **1, 2, 5, 6, 8, 11, 13, 15**
Koeleria macrantha   Crested hair-grass   **8**
Trisetum flavescens   Yellow oat-grass   **7, 8**
Deschampsia cespitosa
   Tufted hair-grass   **1-3, 7-9, 11, 12, 14, 15**
Aira praecox   Early hair-grass   **1, 8**
A. caryophyllea   Silver hair-grass   **1, 8**
Anthoxanthum odoratum   Sweet vernal-grass   **1, 7-9, 12**
Holcus lanatus   Yorkshire-fog   **1, 2, 4, 7, 8, 11, 12, 15**
H. mollis   Creeping soft-grass   **7-9, 11, 13**
Agrostis canina   Brown bent   **1, 7**
A. capillaris   Common bent   **1, 4, 7-9**
A. gigantea   Black bent   **1**
A. stolonifera   Creeping bent   **1, 2, 4, 8, 11, 15**
Calamagrostis epigejos
   Wood small-reed   **4, 7, 8, 14, 15, 17**
Phleum pratense ssp. *pratense*
   Timothy-grass   **1, 3, 5-8, 15**
P. pratense ssp. *bertolonii*   Cat's-tail   **1, 7, 8**
Alopecurus pratensis   Meadow foxtail   **1-3, 5, 8, 9, 15**
A. myosuroides   Black-grass   **1, 9**
Phalaris arundinacea   Reed canary-grass   **8**
P. canariensis   Canary-grass   **7, 8**
Milium effusum   Wood millet   **7, 11**
Phragmites australis   Common reed   **4, 8**
Molinia caerula   Purple moor-grass   **8**
* *Nardus stricta*   Mat-grass   **1** (1886)
ARACEAE
Arum maculatum   Cuckoo pint   **1, 2, 7-9, 11-17**

Vascular Plants

LEMNACEAE
Lemna trisulca   Ivy-leaved duckweed   **13**
L. minor   Common duckweed   **7-9, 13**
SPARGANIACEAE
Sparganium erectum   Branched bur-reed   **7**
TYPHACEAE
Typha latifolia   Bulrush   **8, 9, 13**
CYPERACEAE
Scirpus lacustris   Common club-rush   **9, 13**
* *S. setaceus*   Bristle club-rush   **1** (1886)
* *Blysmus compressus*   Flat-sedge   **1** (1831 Baxter)
* *Eriophorum angustifolium*   Common cottongrass   **8**
   (1926 Druce)
* *E. latifolium*   Broad-leaved cottongrass   **8** (1926 Druce)
Eleocharis palustris   Common spike-rush   **7**
Schoenus nigricans   Black bog-rush   **8**
Carex paniculata   Greater tussock sedge   **8**
C. otrubae   False fox sedge   **1, 5, 7, 11, 15**
C. muricata   Prickly sedge   **2**
* *C. divulsa*   Grey sedge   **1, 8** (1886)
* *C. disticha*   Brown sedge   **8** (1974)
C. remota   Remote sedge   **1, 7-9, 11, 13-15**
C. ovalis   Oval sedge   **1, 7**
* *C. echinata*   Star sedge   **8** (1974)
* *C. dioica*   Dioecious sedge   **8** (1926)
C. hirta   Hairy sedge   **1, 2, 5, 7**
C. acutiformis   Lesser pond sedge   **7, 8, 11, 13**
C. riparia   Greater pond-sedge   **14**
C. vesicaria   Bladder-sedge   **13**
C. pendula   Pendulous sedge   **15**
C. sylvatica   Wood-sedge   **1, 7-17**
C. strigosa   Thin-spiked wood-sedge   **9-11**
C. flacca   Glaucous sedge   **1, 8, 14, 15**
* *C. panicea*   Carnation sedge   **8** (1974)
* *C. binervis*   Green-ribbed sedge   **8** (1864 Dyer)
C. lepidocarpa   Long-stalked yellow-sedge   **8**
C. pallescens   Pale sedge   **14, 15**
C. caryophyllea   Spring-sedge   **6-8**
C. pilulifera   Pill sedge   **1, 8**
C. nigra   Common sedge   **8**
C. pulicaris   Flea sedge   **1, 8**
ORCHIDACEAE
Epipactis palustris   Marsh helleborine   **8, 13**
E. helleborine   Broad-leaved helleborine   **1, 7**
E. purpurata   Violet helleborine   **7, 11**
E. phyllanthes   Green-flowered helleborine   **8**
* *Cephalanthera damasonium*   White helleborine   **1**
   (1886)
* *Neottia nidus-avis*
   Bird's-nest orchid   **8** (c. 1920 Dr. Schonland)
Listera ovata   Common twayblade   **1, 7, 8, 12**
* *Spiranthes spiralis*   Autumn lady's-tresses   **1** (1833)
* *Platanthera chlorantha*
   Greater butterfly-orchid   **11** (c. 1970)
Gymnadenia conopsea   Fragrant orchid   **8**
* *Coeloglossum viride*   Frog orchid   **1** (Sibthorp)
* *Dactylorhiza incarnata*
   Early marsh-orchid   **8** (H. Boswell)
* *D. majalis ssp. praetermissa*
   Southern marsh-orchid   **8** (1974)
D. fuchsii
   Common spotted-orchid   **1,3,4,7,8,11,12,15**

* *Orchis morio*   Green-winged orchid   **5** (1980)
   O. mascula   Early purple-orchid   **8, 11, 12, 14, 15**
* *Ophrys sphegodes*   Early spider-orchid   **1** (1806)
   O. apifera   Bee orchid   **8**

* Species not recorded since 1980.
Nomenclature after Tutin et al. (1964-80) Flora Europaea. C.U.P.
English names after Dony, Rob & Perring's English names of
wild flowers.

Bee orchid (Ophrys apifera)

Appendix 6

Orthoptera

ACRIDIDAE
Chorthippus brunneus   Common field grasshopper   **2,8**
C. parallelus   Meadow grasshopper   **2,8**
TETRIGIDAE
* *Tetrix subulata*   Slender groundhopper   **7**
TETTIGONIDAE
Leptophyes punctatissima   Speckled bush cricket   **8**
Pholidoptera griseoaptera   Dark bush cricket   **2,7,8**
Meconema thalassinum   Oak bush cricket   **7,8**
Metrioptera brachyptera   Bog bush cricket   **8**

*   Species not recorded since 1980
Nomenclature after Kloet, G.S. and Hinks, W.D. (1964) A
check list of British Insects. 1. Small Orders. R.E.S.

   Speckled bush cricket (Leptophyes punctatissima)

Odonata

The dragonfly fauna of Shotover is rather disappointing although it is possible that other interesting species have been missed. The old record for *Gomphus* must be considered doubtful because of the lack of rivers which provide its normal habitat. The *Orthetrum coerulescens* recorded in 1983 from the fen at Sydling's Copse is noteworthy. The most widely seen dragonflies are *Aeshna grandis* and *Sympetrum striolatum* both of which are often seen far from water from July to September. All other species occur in good numbers near the more open ponds at Shotover.

COENAGRIDAE
Ischnura elegans   **1**
Coenagrion puella   **1**
Pyrrhosoma nymphula   **8**
GOMPHIDAE
* *Gomphus vulgatissimus*   (seen only)
AESHNIDAE
Aeshna grandis   **1,7,8**
A. juncea   **1,8**
A. mixta   **1,7,8**
A. cyanea   **8**
LIBELLULIDAE
Orthetrum coerulescens   **8**
Libellula depressa   **1**
L. quadrimaculata   **1**
Sympetrum striolatum   **1**

*Species not recorded since 1980
Nomenclature after Kloet, G.S. and Hinks, W.D. (1964). A
check.list of British Insects. 1 Small Orders. R.E.S.

Brown hawker (Aeshna grandis)

Coleoptera

A substantial list of beetles has been compiled and it is certain that a great many more remain to be found. Several local and uncommon species are present including *Rhizophagus nitidulus* (a small, dead wood feeder), two local longhorns (*Agapanthia villosoviridescens* and *Phytoecia cylindrica*) and a local dor beetle *Typhaeus typhoeus*. Several rare beetles were recorded pre-1930 which have not been seen in recent years. Of particular note are the ground beetle *Harpalus honestus*, the oil beetle *Meloe rugosus*, the rove beetle *Aleochara maculata* and the Pselaphid *Claviger longicomis*. Other local ground beetles which have not been recorded in recent years are *Notiophilus aquaticus*, *Dyschirius politus*, *Panageus bipustulatus* and *Metabletus truncatellus* – it is interesting that these are all insects of open country.

One disappointment is the shortage of noteworthy dead wood beetles at Shotover. The dead wood species are mostly common (e.g. *Tetratoma fungorum*, *Mycetophagus bipustulatus* and *Atrecus baptolinus*) whereas Oxfordshire's other Royal Forests (Wychwood and Woodstock Chase) boast a range of rarities.

CARABIDAE
Cicindela campestris
Carabus nemoralis **7**
C. violaceus **1, 7**
* *C. monilis*
* *C. problematicus*
Cychrus rostratus **7**
Leistus ferrugineus **7**
L. fulvibarbis **7**
L. rufomarginatus **7**
Nebria brevicollis **1, 7**
Notiophilus biguttatus **1, 7**
N. substriatus **1**
* *N. aquaticus*
N. palustris **1**
Loricera pilicomis **1, 7**
Clivinia fossor **7**
Trechus quadristriatus **1, 7**
T. obtusus **1, 7**
T. secalis **1, 7**
* *Dyschirius politus*
* *Patrobus atrorufus*
Asaphidion flavipes **7**
Bembidion lampros **7**
B. properans **7**
B. tetracolum **7**
B. guttula **1, 7**
* *B. nitidulus*
* *B. articulatum*
Pterostichus madidus **1, 7**
P. melanarius **7**
P. oblongopunctatus **7**
P. strenuus **7**
P. niger **9**
Abax parallelepipidus **1, 7**
Calathus piceus **7**
* *C. ambiguus*
Agonum albipes **7**
A. assimile **7**
A. viduum **7**
* *Amara tibialis*
A. aenea **1**
Harpalus rufipes **1, 7**
H. aenea **1**

H. azureus **7**
* *H. honestus*
H. affinis **1**
H. rubripes **1**
H. rufitarsis **1**
Bradycellus harpalinus **1, 7**
B. sharpi **7**
B. verbasci **1, 7**
B. ruficollis **1**
Dromius linearis **1**
* *Badister bipustulatus*
* *Panageus bipustulatus*
* *Chlaenius vestitus*
* *Lebia chlorocephala*
* *Metabletus truncatellus*
DYTYSCIDAE
* *Agabus didymus*
Ilybius fuliginosus **1**
HYDROPHILIDAE
* *Cercyon atomarius*
* *C. marinus*
* *C. unipunctatus*
Sphaeridium scarabaeoides **1**
Anaceana globulus **7**
Helophorus grandis **7**
LEIODIDAE
Leiodes dubia **7**
L. parvula **7**
L. calcarata **1, 7**
Anistoma humeralis **1, 7**
Amphicyllis globus **7**
Sciodrepoides watsoni **7**
S. fumata **7**
* *Agathidium convexum*
* *A. rotundatum*
Colon brunneum **1, 7**
Nargus wilkini **7**
LEPTINIDAE
* *Leptinus testaceus*
HISTERIDAE
* *Grammostethus marginatus*
* *Peranus bimaculatus*
SILPHIDAE
Nicrophorus humator **1, 7**

N. investigator **1, 7**
N. vespilloides **7**
Necrodes littoralis **1, 7**
Silpha atrata **7**
STAPHYLINIDAE
Micropeplus fulvus **7**
Megarthrus sinuatocollis **7**
* *Proteinus crenulatus* **•**
P. brachypterus **7**
Anthobium atrocephalum **7**
Olophrum piceum **7**
Eusphalerum luteum **1**
Phloeostiba plana **7**
* *Acidota cruentata*
* *Acrolocha sulcula*
* *Philorinum sordidum*
* *Phloeocharis subtilissima*
* *Pseudopsis sulcata*
* *Bledius femoralis*
* *B. gallicus*
* *B. longulus*
* *B. opacus*
Anotylus rugosus **1, 7**
A. sculpturatus **7**
Oxytelus sculptus **7**
* *Oxyporus rufus*
* *Stenus comma*
S. rogeri **7**
* *Lathrobium geminum*
L. multipunctum **7**
L. brunnipes **7**
* *Medon castaneus*
* *Scopaeus sulcicollis*
* *Rugilus erichsoni*
Othius myrmecophilus **7**
O. punctulatus **7**
* *O. angustus*
Atrecus affinis **7**
* *Xantholinus laevigatus*
* *Philonthus agilis*
* *P. albipes*
P. cruentatus **1**
P. decorus **7**
P. intermedius **1**

Coleoptera

P. fimetarius **1**
P. marginatus **1**
* *P. puella*
P. politus **1**
P. sanguinolentus **1**
P. splendens **1**
P. succicola **1**
Platydracus stercorarius **1, 7**
* *P. latebricola*
Staphylinus compressus **7**
S. olens **1, 7, 8**
Ontholestes murinus **1**
Quedius fumatus **7**
* *Q. invreae*
Q. boops **1**
Q. fuliginosus **1**
Q. lateralis **1**
* *Q. maurorufus*
Q. nigriceps **1**
* *Q. picipes*
* *Q. scintillans*
Mycetoporus nigricollis **1**
Bolitobius inclinans **1, 7**
Tachyporus pallidus **7**
T. nitidulus **7**
* *T. tersus*
Tachinus marginellus **7**
T. pallipes **7**
T. signatus **7**
Lordithon trinotatus **7**
L. exoletus **7**
Myllaena dubia **7**
* *M. brevicornis*
* *M. elongata*
* *M. gracilis*
* *M. intermedia*
* *Gyrophaena latissima*
* *G. minima*
Bolitochara bella **7**
Autalia impressa **7**
Cordalia obscura **7**
* *Tachyusa constricta*
* *T. leucopus*
* *T. scitula*
Platarea brunnea **7**
Acrotona fungi **7**
* *Notothecta confusa*
* *Atheta hepatica*

* *Aleuonota gracilenta*
* *Alianta incana*
Drusilla canaliculata **1**
* *Lomechusa emarginata*
* *Ocalea badia*
Phloeopora testacea **7**
Oxypoda altemans **7**
* *Aleochara maculata*
* *A. spadicea*
A. ruficornis **7**
PSELAPHIDAE
Bryaxis puncticollis **7**
* *Claviger longicornis*
Pselaphus heisei **7**
LUCANIDAE
* *Lucanus cervus*
Dorcus parallelepipidus **7**
GEOTRUPIDAE
Geotupes stercorarius **1, 7**
Typhaeus typhoeus **1**
SCARABAEIDAE
Aphodius rufipes **1**
* *A. rufus*
* *A. foetens*
* *A. granarius*
Serica brunnea **1**
Amphimallon solstitialis **1**
Melolontha melolontha **1, 7**
BYRRHIDAE
Byrrhus pilula **1, 7**
HETEROCERIDAE
* *Heterocerus fenestratus*
* *H. marginatus*
Limnichius pygmaeus **1**
ELATERIDAE
Agriotes pallidulus **1, 7**
A. acuminatus **1, 7**
Adrastus pallens **7**
Prostemon tesselatus **1**
* *Ctenicera cuprea*
Dolopius marginatus **7**
Denticollis linearis **1, 7**
Athous haemorrhoidalis **1**
CANTHARIDAE
Rhagonycha femoralis **1, 7**
R. lignosa **1**
R. fulva **1, 2, 7, 8**
Cantharis nigricans **1**
C. lateralis **1**
C. decipiens **1**
C. rufa **1**
C. pellucida **1**
C. cryptica **1**
LAMPYRIDAE
Lampyris noctiluca **8**
MELYRIDAE
Dasytes aeratus **7**
Malachius bipustulatus **1**
CLERIDAE
Thanasimus formicarius **1**
NITIDULIDAE
Meligethes aeneus **1**

M. flavinimus **1**
M. fulvipes **1**
* *M. obscurus*
* *M. solidus*
* *M. umbrosus*
M. rufipes **1**
RHIZOPHAGIDAE
Rhizophagus nitidulus **7**
CRYPTOPHAGIDAE
Cryptophagus saginatus **7**
* *C. pubescens*
Micrambe villosus **1**
Caenoscelis ferruginea **1**
BYTURIDAE
Byturus tomentosus **7**
PYROCHROIDAE
Pyrochroa serraticomis **1, 7**
P. coccinea **7, 8**
COCCINELLIDAE
Chilocorus renipustulatus **1, 7, 8**
Exochomus 4-pustulatus **1, 7, 8**
* *Antisosticta 19-punctata*
Aphidecta obliterata **1**
Tytthaspis sedecimpunctata **7**
Adalia bipunctata **1, 7, 8**
A. 10-punctata **7**
Coccinella 7-punctata **1-17**
C. 11-punctata **7**
Propylea 14-punctata **7**
Anatis ocellata **1**
Calvia 14-punctata **1, 7**
Thea 22-punctata **1**
Propylea 14-punctata **1-17**
Psyllobora 22-punctata **1**
ENDOMYCHIDAE
Endomychus coccineus **7**
LATHRIDIIDAE
Aridius bifasciatus **7**
A. nodifer **7**
Enicmus histrio **7**
E. transversus **1, 7**
CISIDAE
Cis pygmaeus **1**
C. nitidus **7**
MYCETOPHAGIDAE
Typhaea stercorea **1**
Mycetophagus quadripustulatus **1**
TENEBRIONIDAE
Blaps mucronata **1, 7**
* *Tribolium confusum*
TETRATOMIDAE
Tetratoma fungorum **1**
MELANDRYIDAE
Orchesia undulata **1, 7**
SCRAPTIDAE
* *Anaspis thoracica*
A. frontalis **1**
A. garneysi **1**
MELOIDAE
* *Meloe rugosus*
ANTHICIDAE
* *Notoxus monoceros*

Cardinal beetle (Pyrochroa serraticomis)

CERAMBYCIDAE
Clytus arietis **1, 7**
Tetropium gabrieli **1**
Agapanthia villosoviridescens **2**
Phytoecia cylindrica **1**
Stenocorus meridianus **1**
Strangalia melaneura **8**
S. maculata **2, 8**
BRUCHIDAE
Bruchus rufipes **1**
CHRYSOMELIDAE
Oulema melanopa **1, 7**
Timarcha tenebricosa **1, 2, 7, 8**
* *T. goettingensis*
Crioceris asparagi **7**
Chrysolina polita **1, 2, 7, 8**
C. menthastri **1**
* *C. oricalcia*
Phaedon tumidulus **1**
Plagiodera versicolora **1**
Phyllodecta vitellinae **1**
P. vulgatissima **7**
Phytodecta decemnotata **2**
Sermylassa halensis **1**
Altica brevicollis **2**
Chalcoides aurea **1, 2, 7**
C. aurata **2**
Chaetocnema hortensis **7**
Aphthona coerulea **1**
Sphaeroderma testaceum **2**
* *Galeruca tanaceti*
* *Calomicrus circumfusus*
Longitarsus luridus **7**
L. membranaceus **1**
Psylloides chrysocephala **1**
ATTELABIDAE
Rhynchites germanicus **1**
R. cavifrons **1**
Deporaus betulae **1**
APIONIDAE
* *Apion sanguineum*
* *A. cineraceum*
* *A. seniculus*
* *A. ebeninum*
* *A. striatum*
* *A. aethiops*
* *A. ervi*
* *A. loti*
* *A. reflexum*
A. miniatus **1**
* *A. simile*
A. ulicis **1**
* *A. virens*
* *A. craccae*
* *A. subulatum*
* *A. dissimile*
* *A. varipes*
CURCULIONIDAE
Barypeithes araneiformis **7**
B. pellucidus **7**
Strophosomus capitatus **7**
Barynotus moerens **7**

Leiosoma deflexum **7**
Grypus equiseti **7**
Rhynchaenus rusci **7**
* *R. salicis*
Curculio glandium **1**
C. venosus **7**
Anthonomus ulmi **1**
Otiorhynchus singularis **1**
Cneorhinus plumbeus **1**
Phyllobius maculicornis **1**
P. viridiaeris **1**
P. parvulus **1**
P. pomaceus **1, 7**
P. pyri **1**
P. roberetanus **1**
Polydrusus cervinus **1**
* *Trachyphloeus aristatus*
* *T. bifoveolatus*
* *T. scabriculus*
* *Sitona humeralis*
S. linearis **1**
* *S. lepidus*
S. puncticollis **1**
* *S. macularius*
* *S. sulcifrons*
* *Clenonus piger*
* *Hypera punctata*
* *H. venusta*
* *Alophus triguttatus*
* *Dorytomus validirostris*
* *Coeliodes rubicundus*
* *Ceuthorhynchidius barnevillei*
* *Ceutorhynchus triangulum*
* *Phytobius canaliculatus*
* *Orobitis cyaneus*
* *Tychius meliloti*
SCOLYTIDAE
Scolytus scolytus **1, 7**

* Species not recorded since 1980.
Nomenclature after Kloet, G. S. and
Hinks, W. D. (1977) A Check List of
British Insects. 3. Coleoptera. R.E.S.

*Bloody-nose beetle (*Timarcha tenebricosa*)*

Appendix 9

Diptera

Many rare flies have been recorded from Shotover. Of the old records there are the rare woodland species *Tipula truncorum, T. peliostigma, Ormosia bicornis* and *Criorhina asilica;* rare heathland and rough pasture species such as *Limonia masoni, Asilus crabroniformis, Eudorylas terminalis, Platycheirus discimanus, Volucella inanis* and *Miltogramma gemmari,* the latter two species being associated with solitary bees and wasps; and rare wetland species such as *Stratiomys furcata, Ulidia erythrophthalma* and *Sapromyza bipunctata.* Three rare Shotover flies have not been recorded from Britain in recent years – *Pipizella maculipennis, Eccoptomera ornata* and *Ceromya monstrosicornis.* Very little attention has been paid to the flies recently but species of note from the 1980s are *Stratiomys potamida, Oxycera pulchella, Calliopum elisae* and *Cerodontha hennigi* which mines wood small-reed *(Calamagrostis epigejos).*

The number of rare flies recorded from Shotover is quite outstanding. However, most of the records are more than fifty years old and the rarities may now be extinct. Nevertheless, much suitable habitat remains and a concerted search may well reveal interesting species.

TRICHOCERIDAE
* *Trichocera major*
* *T. saltator*
  T. annulata **7**
  T. hiemalis **8**
TIPULIDAE
* *Tipula truncorum*
  T. meigeni
* *T. scripta*
* *T. cava*
* *T. fascipennis*
  T. obsoleta **8**
* *T. peliostigma*
  T. varipennis **7**
  T.pruinosa **8**
* *Limonia macrostigma*
* *L. masoni*
  L. nubeculosa **1,7,8**
* *L. nigropunctata*
* *L. stigma*
* *L. autumnalis*
* *L. modesta*
* *L. sericata*
  L. tripunctata **7**
* *Pseudolimnophila sepium*
* *Limnophila ferruginea*
  Paradelphomyia dalei **8**
* *Pilaria discicollis*
* *Erioptera stictica*
* *E. griseipennis*
* *E. areolata*
* *Ormosia bicornis*
* *O. hederae*
* *Molophilus flavus*
PSYCHODIDAE
* *Pericoma blandula*
* *P. cognata*
* *P. gracilis*
* *P. neglecta*
* *P. pulchra*
* *Telmatoscopus ambiguus*
* *T. fratercula*
* *T. morulus*

* *T. soleatus*
* *T. rothschildii*
* *Mormia caliginosa*
DIXIIDAE
* *Dixa maculata*
* *D. nebulosa*
* *Dixella aestivallis*
CHAOBORIDAE
* *Chaoborus crystallinus*
CULICIDAE
* *Aedes cantans*
* *A. rusticus*
* *A. geniculatus*
* *A. vexans*
* *A. cinereus*
* *Culiseta fumipennis*
* *C. morsitans*
CERATOPOGONIDAE
* *Forcipomyia brevipennis*
* *Atrichopogon appendiculatus*
* *A. minutus*
* *Dasyhelea notata*
* *D. scutellata*
* *Culicoides odibilis*
* *C. pictipennis*
* *Palpomyia fulva*
* *P. nemorivaga*
* *Bezzia flavicornis*
CHIRONOMIDAE
* *Tanypus punctipennis*
* *Ablabesmyia phatta*
* *Cricotopus reversus*
* *C. sylvestris*
* *Orthocladius obtexens*
* *Glyptotendipes pallens*
ANISOPODIDAE
  Sylvicola cinctus **7**
BIBIONIDAE
* *Bibio lanigerus*
* *B. lepidus*
* *B. marci*
  B. nigriventris **7**
* *B. pomonae*

  B. reticulatus **7**
MYCETOPHILIDAE
* *Bolitophila saundersi*
* *B. hybrida*
* *Symmerus annulatus*
* *Macrocera stigmoides*
* *M. vittata*
* *Orfelia flava*
* *Mycomya winnertzi*
* *Apolephthisa subincana*
* *Boletina gripha*
* *Rymosia bifida*
* *Exechia dorsalis*
* *E. fusca*
* *E. parva*
* *Allodia lugens*
* *Cordyla fissa*
* *Dynatosoma fuscicornis*
* *Mycetophila curviseta*
* *M. stolida*
* *Zygomyia notata*
* *Sceptonia concolor*
* *S. nigra*
* *Platurocypta punctum*
* *P. testata*
SCATOPSIDAE
* *Reichertella geniculata*
CECIDOMYIIDAE
* *Planetella extrema*
* *P. funestra*
STRATIOMYIDAE
* *Beris clavipes*
* *B. fuscipes*
* *B. geniculata*
* *Oxycera formosa*
  O. pulchella **1**
* *Microchrysa cyaneiventris*
* *Sargus splendens*
* *Stratiomys furcata*
  S. potamida **7**
RHAGIONIDAE
* *Rhagio lineola*

Diptera

TABANIDAE
* Hybomitra micans
ASILIDAE
* Asilus crabroniformis
* Dysmachus trigonus
* Neoitamus cyanurus
* Leptogaster guttiventris
* Dioctria atricapilla
* D. baumhaueri
THEREVIDAE
* Thereva plebeia
BOMBYLIIDAE
* Bombylius canescens
  B. major **7,8**
EMPIDIDAE
* Drapetis nigritella
* D. ephippiata
* D. graminum
* Tachydromia connexa
* Platypalpus calceatus
  P. agilis **7**
* P. candicans
* P. ciliaris
* P. coarctatus
* P. exilis
* P. fasciatus
* P. flavicornis
* P. maculipes
* P. niger
* P. nigrititarsis
* P. optivus
* P. pallipes
* P. pictitarsis
* P. pulicarius
* P. ruficornis
* P. verralli
  Bicellaria nigra **7**
  B. pilosa **7**
* B. sulcata
* Trichonomyia flavipes
* Trichina clavipes
* Oedalea flavipes
* O. holmgreni
* Microphorus holosericeus
* Gloma fuscipennis
* Rhamphomyia dentipes
* R. tarsata
* R. variabilis

R. anomalipennis **7**
* R. flava
* R. nigripennis
* R. hybotina
* Empis nigritarsis
  E. chioptera **7**
* E. concolor
* E. digramma
* E. punctata
  E. aestiva **7**
  E. tessellata **7**
  E. grisea **7**
  E. albinervis **7**
  E. livida **7**
  E. praevia **7**
  Tachypeza nubila **7**
* Hilara chorica
* H. cornicula
* H. curtisi
* H. flavipes
* H. griseifrons
  H. interstincta **7**
* H. litorea
* H. manicata
* Heleodromia immaculata
* Chelipoda vocatoria
  Phyllodromia melanocephala **7**
* Chelifera precatoria
* Dolichocephala guttata
* D. irrorata
* D. ocellata
  Trichopeza longicornis **7**
DOLICHOPODIDAE
* Dolichopus picipes
* D. trivialis
* Hercostomus nigripennis
* Hypophyllus obscurellus
* Hydrophorus litoreus
* Raphium appendiculatum
* R. auctum
* R. caliginosum
* R. commune
* Syntormon monilis
* S. pallipes
* Sympycnus aenicoxa
* S. desoutteri
PHORIDAE
  Gymnophora arcuata **7**
  G. quartomollis **7**
  Diploneura funebris **7**
  D. nitidula **7**
* Megaselia campestris
* M. pleuralis
* M. minor
  M. altifrons **7**
  M. brevicostalis **7**
  M. giraudii **7**
  M. longicostalis **7**
  Phora edentata **7**
PIPUNCULIDAE
* Verrallia aucta
* V. pilosa

* Pipunculus thomsoni
* Cephalops furcatus
* C. semifumosus
* Eudorylas fuscipes
* E. terminalis
* E. zonatus
SYRPHIDAE
  Syrphus ribesii **1**
* Epistrophe nitidicollis
  E. elegans **1**
  E. grossulariae **7**
* Dasysyrphus albostriatus
* Leucozona laternarius
  L. lucorum **1**
* Melangyna labiatarum
* M. lasiophthalma
* M. umbellatarum
* M. cincta
* Parasyrphus punctulatus
* Xanthogramma citrofasciatum
  X. pedissequum **7**
* Meliscaeva auricollis
  M. cinctella **7**
* Sphaerophoria scripta
  Episyrphus balteatus **7**
  Rhingia campestris **7**
* Crysotoxum arcuatum
* Baccha elongata
* Platycheirus angustatus
* P. discimanus
  P. manicatus **7**
  P. fulviventris **8**
* P. peltatus
  P. scutatus **7**
* Paragus tibialis
* Pipiza bimaculata
* P. fenestrata
* Pipizella maculipennis
* Parapenium flavitarsis
* Cheilosia bergenstammi
* C. honesta
* C. impressa
* C. intonsa
* C. proxima
* C. scutellata
* C. soror
* C. vernalis
* C. vulpina
* Ferdinandea cuprea
* Chrysogaster chalybeata
* C. solstitialis
* C. virescens
* Lejogaster splendida
* Orthonerva splendens
* Eumerus strigatus
* Volucella inanis
* Sericomyia silentis
* Criorhina asilica
* C. berberina
* Merodon equestris
* Helophilus hybridus
* H. parallelus

  Bee-fly (Bombylius major)

Diptera

* *Erastalinus sephulchralis*
  Sphegina verrucunda **8**
  Eristalis pertinax **1,7**
  E. tenax **1,7**
  E. arbustorum **1,7**
  Xylota segnis **7**
  CONOPIDAE
* *Conops ceriaeformis*
* *C. flavipes*
* *C. quadrifasciata*
* *Physocephala rufipes*
* *Myopa buccata*
* *M. fasciata*
* *M. polystigma*
* *Thecophora atra*
* *Sicus ferrugineus*
  TEPHRITIDAE
* *Rhagoletis alternata*
* *Chaetosomella onotrophes*
* *Terellia serratulae*
* *Dithryca guttularis*
* *Oxyna parietina*
* *Tephritis cometa*
* *T. hyoscyami*
  PLATYSTOMATIDAE
* *Rivellia syngenesiae*
  OTTIDAE
* *Ulidia erythrophthalma*
* *Herina frondescentiae*
' *H. germinationis*
* *H. lugubris*
  MICROPEZIDAE
* *Micropeza corrigiolata*
* *Calobata ephippium*
  PSILIDAE
* *Loxocera albiseta*
* *Psila atra*
  CHAMAEMYIIDAE
* *Chamaemyia fasciata*
* *C. polystigma*
  LAUXANIIDAE
* *Trigonometopus frontalis*
* *Minettia fasciata*
  M. longipennis **7**
* *M. plumicornis*
* *M. rivosa*
* *Sapromyza bipunctata*
* *S. obsoleta*
* *Peplomyza litura*
* *Aulogastromyia anisodactyla*
* *Lyciella decempunctata*
* *L. decipiens*
* *L. pallidiventris*
  L. rorida **7**
* *Homoneura tesquae*
  Calliopum elisae **8**
  C. geniculatum **7**
  HELEOMYZIDAE
* *Suilla bicolor*
  S. affinis **7**
* *Allophyla atricornis*
* *Eccoptomera microps*

* *E. ornata*
* *Scoliocentra scutellaris*
  SEPSIDAE
* *Saltella sphondylli*
* *Themira annulipes*
* *Sepsis punctum*
  SCIOMYZIDAE
* *Pherbellia albocostata*
* *P. dorsata*
* *P. dubia*
* *P. pallidiventris*
* *P. scutellaris*
* *P. ventralis*
  Coremacera tristis **1**
* *Dichetophora obliterata*
* *Elgiva sundewalli*
* *Hydromya dorsalis*
* *Tetanocera ferruginea*
  T. silvatica **8**
  Limnia paludicola **8**
  SPHAEROCERIDAE
* *Sphaerocera denticulata*
* *S. pallidiventris*
* *Coproyza flavipennis*
* *C. costalis*
* *C. uncinata*
* *Leptocera appendiculata*
* *L. bifrons*
* *L. denticulata*
* *L. flavipes*
* *L. vitripennis*
* *L. ochripes*
* *L. lugubris*
* *L. pseudolugubris*
  PALLOPTERIDAE
* *Palloptera arcuata*
* *P. saltuum*
  LONCHAEIDAE
* *Lonchaea fumosa*
* *L. sylvatica*
  OPOMYZIDAE
* *Opomyza florum*
  CARNIIDAE
* *Meonura flavifacies*
  ANTHOMYZIDAE
* *Paranthomyza nitida*
  ASTEIIDAE
* *Leiomyza laevigata*
  CAMILLIDAE
* *Camilla glabra*
  EPHYDRIDAE
* *Athyroglossa glabra*
* *Discomyza incurva*
* *Psilopa nitidula*
* *Trimerina madizans*
* *Notiphila cinerea*
* *Philygria posticata*
* *P. stictica*
* *Nostima picta*
* *Parydra fossarum*
* *Hyadina guttata*
* *H. nitida*

* *Pelina aenea*
* *P. aenescens*
* *Limnellia quadrata*
* *Scatophila caviceps*
* *S. variegata*
  DIASTATIDAE
* *Campichoeta obscuripennis*
  C. basalis **8**
* *Diastata fuscula*
* *D. inornata*
* *D. unipunctata*
  DROSOPHILIDAE
* *Scaptomyza graminum*
  Drosophila fenestratum **8**
* *D. obscura*
* *D. tristis*
  MILICHIIDAE
* *Madiza glabra*
  AGROMYZIDAE
* *Melanagromyza cunctans*
* *Liriomyza orbona*
* *Cerodontha luctuosa*
* *C. hammi*
  C. hennigi **8**
  CHLOROPIDAE
* *Dicraeus raptus*
* *D. tibialis*
* *D. vagans*
* *Elachiptera megaspis*
* *E. tuberculifera*
* *Meromyza saltatrix*
* *M. variegata*
* *Lasiosina approximatonervis*
* *Cetema myopina*
* *Chlorops hypostigma*
* *C. rufina*
* *C. serena*
* *Thaumatomyia hallandica*
* *T. trifasciata*
  TACHINIDAE
* *Alophora obesa*
* *Dexia rustica*
* *Macquartia tenebricosa*
* *Solieria fenestrata*
* *S. inanis*
* *Elfia cingulata*
* *Ceromya monstrosicornis*
* *Masicera pavoniae*
  SARCOPHAGIDAE
* *Miltogramma germari*

Syrphus ribesii

Diptera

* *M. punctatum*
  CALLIPHORIDAE
  Lucilia caesar **1**
  L. illustris **1**
  L. sericata **1**
  Calliphora vicina **1**
  C. vomitoria **1**
  Pollenia rudis **1**
  Phormia terraenovae **1**
  SCATHOPHAGIDAE
* *Norellisoma lituratum*
* *Cordilura pubera*
* *Nanna fasciata*
* *N. tibiella*
  ANTHOMYIIDAE
* *Chirosia parvicornis*
* *Myopina myopina*
* *Pegohlemyia fugax*
* *Paraprosalpia billbergi*
* *Anthomyia imbrida*
* *Phorbia sepia*
* *Leucophora sociata*
* *L. sponsa*
* *Delia criniventris*
* *D. frontella*
* *Egle parva*
* *Pegomyza praepotens*
* *Pegomya nigrisquama*
  FANNIIDAE
* *Fannia armata*
* *F. hamata*
* *F. mollissima*
* *F. mutica*
* *F. polychaeta*
* *F. scalaris*
* *F. serena*
  F. sociella **7**
  MUSCIDAE
* *Thricops nigrifrons*
* *T. semicinerea*
* *Drymeia hamata*
* *Ophyra capensis*
* *Phaonia incana*
* *P. populi*
* *P. signata*
* *P. trimaculata*
* *Helina atripes*
* *H. duplicata*
* *Hebecnema vespertina*
* *Mydaea scutellaris*
* *M. urbana*
* *Limnophora maculosa*
* *Lispe tentaculata*
* *Spanochaeta dorsalis*
* *Coenosia intermedia*
* *C. lineatipes*

* Species not recorded since 1980.
Nomenclature after Kloet, G.S. and
Hinks, W.D. (1975). A check list of
British Insects. 5. Diptera. R.E.S.

Appendix 10

Butterflies

The neighbouring Bernwood Forest possesses one of the richest butterfly communities in Britain and it is not surprising that a lot of interest is found in the Shotover woods. All of the hairstreaks have been recorded although the elusive brown hairstreak has not been seen in recent years. Of the *Nymphalidae*, white admirals are probably found in all of the woods, purple emperors in a few of the woods and the very rare large tortoiseshell has been recorded from both Shotover Hill and Brasenose Wood since the 1960s.

Sydling's Copse has a flourishing colony of dark green fritillaries and, until the late 1970s, a strong colony of white letter hairstreaks. In addition there were records of pearl-bordered fritillary, marsh fritillary and small blue in 1976. None of these butterflies have been seen in subsequent years and so were probably vagrants responding to the abnormally hot summer that year.

Three butterflies which are extinct from Shotover are Duke of Burgundy, small blue and chalkhill blue. The Duke of Burgundy was probably found in a sheltered pasture on the south side of Shotover Hill which was converted to arable in the 1950s. Chalkhill and small blues were found in unimproved grassland to the north of the Bayswater Brook which was ploughed some time after 1949.

HESPERIIDAE
Thymelicus sylvestris   Small skipper   **1, 2, 7, 8**
Ochlodes venata   Large skipper   **1, 2, 7, 8**
PIERIDAE
Gonepteryx rhamni   The brimstone   **1, 2, 7, 8, 15**
Pieris brassicae   Large white   **1, 2, 7, 8, 15**
P. rapae   Small white   **1, 2, 7, 8, 15**
P. napi   Green-veined white   **1, 2, 7, 8, 15**
Anthocharis cardamines   Orange-tip   **1, 2, 7, 8, 15**
Colias croceus   Clouded yellow   **6, 8** (1983)
Leptidea sinapsis   Wood white   **15**
LYCAENIDAE
Quercusia quercus   Purple hairstreak   **1, 7, 8**
Strymonidia pruni   Black hairstreak   **7, 15**
S. w-album   White-letter hairstreak   **8**
Callophrys rubi   Green hairstreak   **7, 8**
* *Thecla betulae*   Brown hairstreak   **1**
Aricia agestis   Brown argus   **8**
Lycaena phlaeas   Small copper   **1, 2, 7, 8**
Polyommatus icarus   Common blue   **1, 2, 7, 8**
Celastrina argiolus   Holly blue   **1, 7, 8**
* *Lysandra coridon*   Chalkhill blue   **6** (1949)
* *Cupido minimus*   Small blue   **6** (1949), **8** (1976)
RIODINIDAE
* *Hamearis lucina*   Duke of Burgundy   **1**
NYMPHALIDAE
Vanessa atalanta   Red admiral   **1, 2, 7, 8**
Cynthia cardui   Painted lady   **1, 8**
Ladoga camilla   White admiral   **1, 7, 8, 14, 15**
Apatura iris   Purple emperor   **7, 14, 15**
Aglais urticae   Small tortoiseshell   **1-17**
* *Nymphalis polychloros*
    Large tortoiseshell   **1** (1976), **7** (1962)
Inachis io   Peacock   **1-17**
Polygonia c-album   The comma   **1, 2, 7, 8, 15**
Argynnis aglaja   Dark green fritillary   **8**
* *Boloria euphrosyne*
    Pearl-bordered fritillary   **8** (once only 1976)
* *Eurodryas aurinia*   Marsh fritillary   **8** (once only 1976)
SATYRIDAE
Lasiommata megera   The wall   **1, 2, 7, 8**

Pararge aegeria   Speckled wood   **1, 2, 7-13, 15**
Melanargia galathea   Marbled white   **1, 2, 8**
Pyronia tithonus   Hedge brown   **1,2,7,8,15**
Maniola jurtina   Meadow brown   **1,2,6-8,15**
Aphantopus hyperantus   Ringlet   **1, 2, 7, 8**
Coenonympha pamphilus   Small heath   **1, 2, 8**

* Species not recorded since 1980.
Nomenclature after Bradley, J. D. and Fletcher, D. S. (1979)
British Butterflies and Moths. Curwen Books.

Appendix 11

Moths

The 260 recorded species of moth include many which are confined to woodland. Local woodland moths include the sprawler (*Brachionycha sphinx*), scarce silver lines (*Pseudoips bicolorana*) and dotted rustic (*Rhyacia simulans*). Two uncommon woodland species which have not been recorded in recent years are the broad-bordered bee hawk (*Hemaris fuciformis*) and the oak nycteoline (*Nycteola revayana*). Other species of note are the archer's dart (*Agrotis vestigialis*) which is a mainly coastal moth and the forester (*Procris statices*) which is a nationally declining moth usually found in old meadows.

HEPIALIDAE
Hepialus humuli Ghost **7, 8**
H. sylvina Orange swift **7, 8**
H. lupulinus Common swift **7**
COSSIDAE
Zeuzera pyrina Leopard moth **7, 8**
ZYGAENIDAE
Zygaena filipendulae Six-spot burnet **7, 8**
Z. lonicerae Narrow-bordered five-spot burnet **7, 8**
* *Procris statices* The forester **7** (3 July 1971)
LASIOCAMPIDAE
Philudoria potatoria The drinker **7, 8**
Malacosoma neustria Lackey **7, 8**
Poecilocampa populi December moth **7**
Trichiura crataegi Pale eggar **8**
DREPANIDAE
Cilix glaucata Chinese character **7**
Drepana binaria Oak hook-tip **7, 8**

D. falcataria Pebble hook-tip **7, 8**
THYATIRIDAE
Tethea ocularis Figure of eighty **7**
Achlya flavicornis Yellow-horned **7**
Habrosyne pyritoides Buff arches **7, 8**
Thyatira batis Peach blossom **7, 8**
GEOMETRIDAE
Archiearis parthenias Orange underwing **7**
Alsophila aescularia March moth **7**
Pseudopterpna pruinata Grass emerald **7, 8**
Geometra papilionaria Large emerald **7, 8**
Comibaena bajularia Blotched emerald **7, 8**
Hemithea aestivaria Common emerald **7, 8**
Hemistola chrysoprasaria Small emerald **8**
Cyclophora punctaria Maiden's blush **7**
Timandra griseata Blood-vein **7, 8**
Scopula imitaria Small blood-vein **7**
Idaea aversata Riband wave **7, 8**
I. dimidiata Single-dotted wave **7**
Xanthorhoe ferrugata Dark-barred twin-spot carpet **7, 8**
X. spadicearia Red twin-spot carpet **7, 8**
X. fluctuata Garden carpet **7, 8**
X. montanata Silver-ground carpet **7, 8**
Scotopteryx chenopodiata Shaded broad-bar **7, 8**
Epirrhoe alternata Common carpet **7, 8**
Ecliptopera silaceata Small phoenix **7, 8**
Eulithis pyraliata Barred straw **7, 8**
Thera obeliscata Grey pine carpet **7**
Hydriomena furcata July high flyer **7, 8**
Cidaria fulvata Barred yellow **8**
Colostygia pectinataria Green carpet **8**
Triphosa dubitata The tissue **8**
* *Odezia atrata* Chimney sweeper
Philereme transversata Dark umber **8**
Perizoma alchemillata Small rivulet **8**
* *Electrophaes corylata* Broken-barred carpet
Mesoleuca albicillata Beautiful carpet **8**
Camptogramma bilineata Yellow shell **7, 8**
Cosmorhoe ocellata Purple bar **7, 8**
Larentia clavaria Mallow **7**
Lobophora halterata Seraphim **7**
Eulithis mellinata Spinach **7**
Operophtera brumata Winter **7**
Epirrita dilutata November **7**
Chloroclysta citrata Dark marbled carpet **7, 8**
C. truncata Common marbled carpet **7, 8**
Catarhoe cuculata Royal mantle **8**
Eupithecia centaureata Lime-speck pug **7**
E. icterata Tawny-speckled pug **7**

  Six-spot burnet (Zygaena filipendulae) on common centaury

Moths

Chloroclystis rectangulata   Green pug   **7**
C. v-ata   V-pug   **7**
Aplocera plagiata   Treble-bar   **7**
Abraxas grossulariata   Magpie   **7, 8**
Lomaspilis marginata   Clouded border   **7, 8**
Ligdia adustata   Scorched carpet   **7, 8**
Semiothisa wauaria   V-moth   **7**
S. clathrata   Latticed heath   **7, 8**
S. liturata   Tawny-barred angle   **8**
Petrophora chlorosata   Brown silver-line   **7**
Plagodis dolabraria   Scorched wing   **7**
Opisthograptis luteolata   Brimstone   **7, 8**
Apeira syringaria   Lilac beauty   **8**
Ennomos alniaria   Canary-shouldered thorn   **7, 8**
E. quercinaria   August thorn   **7, 8**
E. fuscantaria   Dusky thorn   **7, 8**
Selenia dentaria   Early thorn   **7, 8**
S. tetralunaria   Purple thorn   **7, 8**
Odontopera bidentata   Scalloped hazel   **7**
Crocallis elinguaria   Scalloped oak   **7, 8**
Colotois pennaria   Feathered thorn   **7**
Ourapteryx sambucaria   Swallow-tailed   **7, 8**
Agriopis leucophaearia   Spring usher   **7**
A. marginaria   Dotted border   **7**
Erannis defoliaria   Mottled umber   **7**
Apocheima pilosaria   Pale brindled beauty   **7**
A. hispidaria   Small brindled beauty   **7**
Lycia hirtaria   Brindled beauty   **7**
Biston betularia   Peppered   **7, 8**
B. strataria   Oak beauty   **7**
Peribatodes rhomboidaria   Willow beauty   **7, 8**
Alcis repandata   Mottled beauty   **7, 8**
Serraca punctinalis   Pale oak beauty   **7**
Aethalura punctulata   Grey birch   **7**
Cabera exanthemata   Common wave   **7**
C. pusaria   Common white wave   **8**
Campaea margaritata   Light emerald   **7, 8**
Ectropis crepuscularia   Small engrailed   **8**
Lomographa bimaculata   White pinion spotted   **8**
L. temerata   Clouded silver   **7, 8**
Ematurga atomaria   Common heath   **7**
SPHINGIDAE
Laothoe populi   Poplar hawk   **7, 8**
Mimas tiliae   Lime hawk   **7**
Smerinthus ocellata   Eyed hawk   **7**
Deilephila elpenor   Elephant-hawk   **7**
D. porcellus   Small elephant-hawk   **7**
* Hemaris fuciformis   Broad-bordered bee hawk   **7**
NOTODONTIDAE
Phalera bucephala   Buff-tip   **7, 8**
Cerura vinula   Puss moth   **7**
Furcula furcula   Sallow kitten   **7**
Notodonta dromedarius   Iron prominent   **7**
Eligmodonta ziczac   Pebble prominent   **7, 8**
Pheosia gnoma   Lesser swallow prominent   **7, 8**
P. tremula   Swallow prominent   **7, 8**
Ptilodon capucina   Coxcomb prominent   **7, 8**
Pterostoma palpina   Pale prominent   **7, 8**
Drymonia dodonaea   Marbled brown   **7**
D. ruficornis   Lunar marbled brown   **7**
Clostera curtula   Chocolate-tip   **7, 8**
Diloba caeruleocephala   Figure of 8   **7**

LYMANTRIIDAE
Orgyia antiqua   Vapourer   **7, 8**
Dasychira pudibunda   Pale tussock   **7**
Euproctis similis   Yellow-tail   **7, 8**
Leucoma salicis   White satin   **7, 8**
ARCTIIDAE
* Nudaria mundana   Muslin footman   **7**
Eilema lurideola   Common footman   **7, 8**
E. griseola   Dingy footman   **8**
Arctia caja   Garden tiger   **7, 8**
Spilosoma lubricipeda   White ermine   **7, 8**
S. luteum   Buff ermine   **7, 8**
Diaphora mendica   Muslin moth   **7**
Phragmatobia fuliginosa   Ruby tiger   **7, 8**
Tyria jacobaeae   Cinnabar   **7, 8**
NOLIDAE
Nola cucullatella   Short cloaked   **8**
NOCTUIDAE
Euxoa nigricans   Garden dart   **7**
Agrotis segetum   Turnip moth   **7, 8**
A. vestigialis   Archer's dart   **8**
A. exclamationis   Heart and dart   **7, 8**
A. ipsilon   Dark sword-grass   **7, 8**
A. puta   Shuttle-shaped dart   **7**
Axylia putris   Flame   **7, 8**
Ochropleura plecta   Flame shoulder   **7, 8**
Noctua pronuba   Yellow underwing   **7**
N. comes   Lesser yellow underwing   **7, 8**
N. fimbriata   Broad-bordered yellow underwing   **7, 8**
N. janthina
   Lesser broad-bordered yellow underwing   **7, 8**
N. interjecta
   Least broad-bordered yellow underwing   **7**
Rhyacia simulans   Dotted rustic   **7**
Graphiphora augur   Double dart   **7, 8**

Diarsia mendica   Ingrailed clay   **8**
D. rubi   Small square-spot   **8**
Xestia c-nigrum   Setaceous hebrew character   **7**
X. triangulum   Double square-spot   **7, 8**
X. sexstrigata   Six-striped rustic   **7, 8**
X. xanthographa   Square-spot rustic   **7, 8**
Anaplectoides prasina   Green arches   **8**
Naenia typica   Gothic   **7**
Cerastis rubricosa   Red chestnut   **7**
Hada nana   Shears   **7**
Polia nebulosa   Grey arches   **7**
P. bombycina   Pale shining brown   **8**
Mamestra brassicae   Cabbage moth   **7, 8**
Melanchra persicariae   Dot moth   **7, 8**
Lacanobia thalassina   Pale-shouldered brocade   **7, 8**
L. oleracea   Bright-line brown-eye   **7, 8**
* *Ceramica pisi*   Broom moth   **7**
Hecatera bicolorata   Broad-barred white   **7**
Hadena rivularis   Campion   **7**
H. compta   Varied coronet   **7**
Cerapteryx graminis   Antler moth   **7**
Tholera decimalis   Feathered gothic   **7**
Orthosia cruda   Small quaker   **7**
O. gracilis   Powdered quaker   **7**
O. stabilis   Common quaker   **7**
O. incerta   Clouded drab   **.7**
O. munda   Twin-spotted quaker   **7**
O. gothica   Hebrew character   **7**
Panolis flammea   Pine beauty   **7**
Mythimna conigera   Brown-line bright-eye   **7, 8**
M. ferrago   Clay   **7, 8**
M. impura   Smoky wainscot   **7**
M. pallens   Common wainscot   **7, 8**

Brachylomia viminalis   Minor shoulder knot   **8**
Cucullia umbratica   Shark   **7**
C. verbasci   Mullein   **8**
Brachionychia sphinx   Sprawler   **7**
Aporophyla lutulenta   Deep-brown dart   **7**
Xylocampa areola   Early grey   **7**
Allophyes oxyacanthae   Green-brindled crescent   **7**
Dichonia aprilina   Merveille du jour   **7**
* *Antitype chi*   Grey chi   **7**
Polymixis flavicincta   Large ranunculus   **7**
Eupsilia transversa   Satellite   **7**
Agrochola lota   Red-line quaker   **7**
A. macilenta   Yellow-line quaker   **7**
A. helvola   Flounced chestnut   **7**
A. litura   Brown-spot pinion   **7**
A. lychnidis   Beaded chestnut   **7**
Atethmia centrago   Centre-barred sallow   **7**
Omphaloscelis lunosa   Lunar underwing   **7**
Xanthia aurago   Barred sallow   **7**
X. icteritia   Sallow   **7**
Acronicta aceris   Sycamore   **7**
A. megacephala   Poplar grey   **7, 8**
A. psi   Grey dagger   **7, 8**
A. rumicis   Knot grass   **7**
Cryphia domestica   Marbled beauty   **7**
Amphipyra tragopoginis   Mouse moth   **7, 8**
A. pyramidea   Copper underwing   **7, 8**
Dipterygia scabriuscula   Bird's wing   **8**
Rusina ferruginea   Brown rustic   **7, 8**
Thalpophila matura   Straw underwing   **7, 8**
Euplexia lucipara   Small angle shades   **7, 8**
Phlogophora meticulosa   Angle shades   **7, 8**
Enargia ypsillon   Dingy shears   **8**
Cosmia trapezina   Dun-bar   **7, 8**
C. pyralina   Lunar-spotted pinion   **7, 8**
* *Panemeria tenebrata*   Small yellow underwing
Apamea monoglypha   Dark arches   **7, 8**
A. lithoxylaea   Light arches   **7, 8**
A. remissa   Dusky brocade   **7**
A. unanimis   Small clouded brindle   **7**
A. anceps   Large nutmeg   **7, 8**
A. sordens   Rustic shoulder-knot   **7**
Mesapamea secalis   Common rustic   **7**
Oligia strigilis   Marbled minor   **8**
O. latruncula   Tawny marbled minor   **8**
Photedes minima   Small dotted buff   **7, 8**
Eremobia ochroleuca   Dusky sallow   **7**
Luperina testacea   Flounced rustic   **7, 8**
Hydraecia micacea   Rosy rustic   **7, 8**
Amphipoea oculea   Ear moth   **7**
Gortyna flavago   Frosted orange   **7**
Charanyca trigrammica   Treble lines   **7**
Hoplodrina alsines   The uncertain   **7**
Caradrina morpheus   Mottled rustic   **7, 8**
C. clavipalpis   Pale mottled willow   **7**
Pseudoips fagana   Green silver-lines   **7**
Bena prasinana   Scarce silver-lines   **7**
Callistege mi   Mother shipton   **7, 8**
Euclidia glyphica   Burnet companion   **7**
Diachrysia chrysitis   Burnished brass   **7, 8**
Polychrysia moneta   Golden plusia   **7**
Autographa gamma   Silver Y   **7**

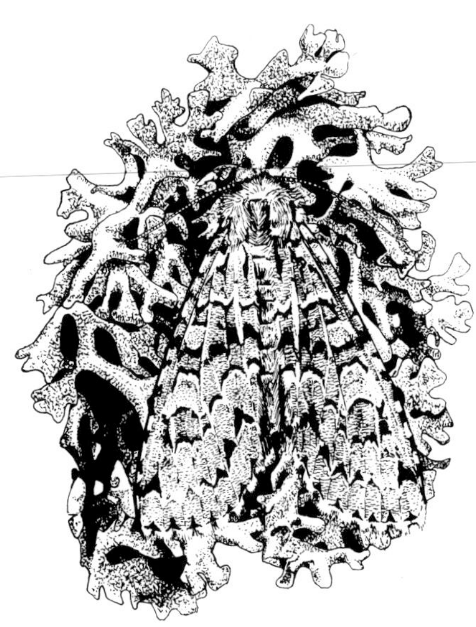

   Merveille du jour (Dichonia aprilina) camouflaged against lichen

Moths

A. pulchrina   Beautiful golden Y   **7, 8**
A. jota   Plain golden Y   **7, 8**
Abrostola triplasia   Spectacle   **7, 8**
* *Nycteola revayana*   Oak nycteoline
Catocala nupta   Red underwing   **7**
Scoliopteryx libatrix   Herald   **7**
Laspeyria flexula   Beautiful hook-tip   **7, 8**
Hypena proboscidalis   Snout   **7, 8**
Herminia tarsipennalis   Fan-foot   **8**
H. nemoralis   Small fan-foot   **8**

* Species not recorded since 1980.
Nomenclature after Bradley, J. D. and Fletcher D. S. (1979)
British Butterflies and Moths. Curwen Books.

Appendix 12

Aculeate Hymenoptera

by C. O'Toole, Hope Department of Entomology, Oxford University

The majority of ants, wasps and bees prefer to nest in sunny situations in dry, sandy, well-drained soils. Although Oxfordshire is not notably rich in such habitats, it is no surprise that the light soils of Shotover support the richest aculeate fauna in the county.

Other aculeate species are adapted for nesting in existing cavities such as beetle borings in dead wood or the soft pith of elder and bramble stems. These species, too, are well-represented at Shotover.

Aculeate species in the following families have been recorded from Shotover:-

	No. species	
Formicidae	8	Ants
Dryinidae	2	
Bethylidae	3	
Chrysididae	8	
Tiphiidae	1	
Mutillidae	1	
Sapygidae	1	Wasps
Pompilidae	12	
Eumenidae	8	
Vespidae	5	
Sphecidae	36	
Colletidae	3	
Andrenidae	30	
Halictidae	20	Bees
Megachilidae	8	
Anthophoridae	15	
Apidae	13	
Total	174	

A breakdown of the present state of our knowledge is as follows:

			Total %
Total number of species recorded	:	174	
Number of species not seen since 1939	:	96	55.2
Number of pre-war records confirmed since 1975	:	48	27.6
Number of species added since 1975	:	30	17.2

Although on paper it appears that 96 species (55.2%) of the recorded total have not been found since 1939, I have only spent three hours collecting at Shotover. In this time, 48 of the pre-war records were confirmed and 30 species were added to the Shotover list. There is no doubt that with more intensive collecting, many of the species recorded before 1939 will be re-discovered.

The consensus among organisers of the Bees, Wasps and Ants Recording and Mapping Scheme

Aculeate Hymenoptera

(BWARMS) is that sites with 150+ species of aculeates are Class 1 in status (G.R. Else, *personal communication*). Thus, Shotover compares favourably with such noted localities as Sandown, Isle of Wight, where 170 were collected in a single day by a BWARMS party and more than favourably with other localities tabled below:-

Locality	No. of recorded species
Ainsdale Sand Dunes NNR (Lancs.)	70
Newborough Warren-Ynys Llanddwyn (Anglesey)	72
Bernwood Forest (Oxon/Bucks.)	94
Dry Sandford Pit (Oxon) (BBONT Reserve)	133
Hitch Copse Pit (Oxon) (BBONT Reserve)	77
Sandown, Isle of Wight	170
Shotover, Oxford	174

Systematic list of aculeate Hymenoptera recorded from Shotover

Many of the records are abstracted from the *Victoria County History of Oxfordshire* and were compiled between the wars by Prof. O.W. Richards and the late A.H. Hamm, when these entomologists were associated with the Hope Department of Entomology. All subsequent records have been added by the author.

DRYINIDAE
* *Chelogynus cameroni*
* *Agonatopoides striatus*
BETHYLIDAE
* *Cephalonomia formiciformis*
* *Bethylus cephalotes*
* *B. fusicornis*
CHRYSIDIDAE
Hedychridium ardens
Chrysis cyanea
* *C. helleni*
* *C. ruddi*
* *C. pustulata*
* *C. viridula*
* *Euchroeus neglectus*
Cleptes semiauratus
TIPHIIDAE
* *Tiphia minuta*
MUTILLIDAE
* *Myrmosa atra*
SAPYGIDAE
Sapyga quinquepunctata
FORMICIDAE
Myrmica rubra
M. sabuleti
* *Leptothorax acervorum*
Formica fusca
Lasius flavus
L. fuliginosus
* *L. mixtus*
L. niger
POMPILIDAE
* *Priocnemis agilis*
* *P. coriacea*
* *P. gracilis*

* *P. parvula*
* *P. pertubator*
* *P. schioedtei*
Pompilus cinereus
* *Arachnospila spissa*
* *A. trivialis*
* *Evagetes crassicornis*
Anoplius viaticus
* *Ceropales maculata*
EUMENIDAE
Odynerus spinipes
Gymnomerus laevipes
* *Ancistrocerus antilope*
A. parietinus
A. scotious
* *Symmorphus connexus*
S. gracilis
* *S. mutinensis*
VESPIDAE
Vespa crabro
Dolichovespula norwegica
* *Vespula germanica*
* *V. rufa*
* *V. vulgaris*
SPHECIDAE
Tachysphex pompiliformis
Trypoxylon attenuatum
Crabro cribrarius
Crossocerus palmipes
* *C. vagabondus*
* *C. varus*
C. dimidiatus
* *C. nigritus*
* *C. capitosus*
Ectemnius cavifrons

E. lapidarius
F. sexcinctus
* *E. continuus*
* *E. rubicola*
Rhopalum clavipes
R. coarctatum
Oxybelus argentatus
* *Mimesa bicolor*
* *Psenulus atratus*
* *Spilomena troglodytes*
Pemphredon lugubris
* *Diodontus luperus*
* *Passaloecus corniger*
* *P. gracilis*
* *P. monilicornis*
Mellinus arvensis
* *M. sabulosa*
* *Nysson dimidiatus*
* *N. interruptus*
N. spinosus
* *Gorytes quadrifasciatus*
* *G. tumidus*
* *Argogorytes fargei*

Lasius fuliginosus

A. mystaceus
Cerceris arenaria
C. rybyensis
COLLETIDAE
Colletes fodiens
Hylaeus communis
* H. cornutus
ANDRENIDAE
* Andrena alfkenella
* A. augustior
* A. spicata
A. barbilabris
A. bicolor
* A. bimaculata
* A. bucephala
A. chrysosceles
A. clarkella
* A. coitana
* A. denticulata
* A. dorsata
* A. flavipes
* A. fucata
A. fulva
A. haemorrhoa
A. helvola
* A. humilis
A. jacobi
* A. labialis
* A. labiata
* A. nigriceps
* A. nigroaenea
* A. niveata
* A. ocreata
* A. praecox
A. saundersella
A. subopaca
A. thoracica
* A. varians
HALICTIDAE
Halictus rubicundus
H. tumulorum
Lasioglossum albipes
L. calceatum
L. fulvicorne
* L. laevigatum
* L. lativentris
L. leucopum
* L. minutissimum
* L. parvulum
* L. punctatissimum
* L. quadrinotatum
L. smeathmanellum
L. villosulum
* Sphecodes crassus
* S. ferruginatus
S. gibbus
* S. hyalinatus
* S. miniatus
S. pellucidus
MEGACHILIDAE
Stelis punctualatissima
Osmia bicolor

O. pilicornis
O. rufa
* Hoplitis spinulosa
* Megachile circumcincta
M. willoughbiella
* Coelioxys elongata
ANTHOPHORIDAE
* Nomada fabriciana
* N. fulvicornis
N. goodeniana
* N. leucophthalma
* N. obtusifrons
* N. panzeri
* N. pleurosticta
* N. ruficornis
* N. rufipes
* N. sheppardana
* N. striata
* Eucera longicornis
Anthophora furcata
* A. retusa
* Melecta albifrons
APIDAE
Bombus hortorum
B. lapidarius
B. lucorum
B. pascuorum
B. pratorum
* B. ruderatus
B. ruderarius
* B. soroeensis
B. terrestris
Psithyrus bohemicus
P. campestris
* P.rupestris
P. vestalis

* Species not recorded since 1980
Nomenclature after Kloet, G.S. and
Hinks, W.D. (1978) A Check List of
British Insects. 4. Hymenoptera. R.E.S.

Bombus lapidarius

Appendix 13

Molluscs

Shotover's molluscs have received very limited attention but the presence of three nationally rare species suggests that further searches may be productive. *Ena montana* is confined to ancient woodland and was recorded at Sydling's Copse in 1975 (T.F. Marshall). *Gyraulus acronicus* is confined to Berkshire and Oxfordshire and was found at Sescut Farm by H.J.M. Bowen in 1974. *Vertigo pusilla* was recorded on a limestone wall near Woodeaton by J. Chatfield in 1968.

   Acanthinula aculeata **8**
   Acicula fusca **8**
   Arion intermedius **8**
   A. ater **7,8**
   Azeca goodalli **8**
   Caecilioides acicula **8**
   Candidula intersecta **8**
   Cepaea hortensis **2**
   C. nemoralis **8**
   Cochlicopa lubrica **8**
   Cochlodina laminata **8**
* *Ena montana* **8** (1975 T.F. Marshall)
   E. obscura **8**
   Euconulus fulvus **8**
* *Gyraulus acronicus* (1974 H.J.M. Bowen)
   Helicella itala **8**
   Limax maximus **8**
   Pomatias elegans **8**
   Vallonia excentrica **8**
* *Vertigo pusilla* (1968 J. Chatfield)

* Species not recorded since 1980.

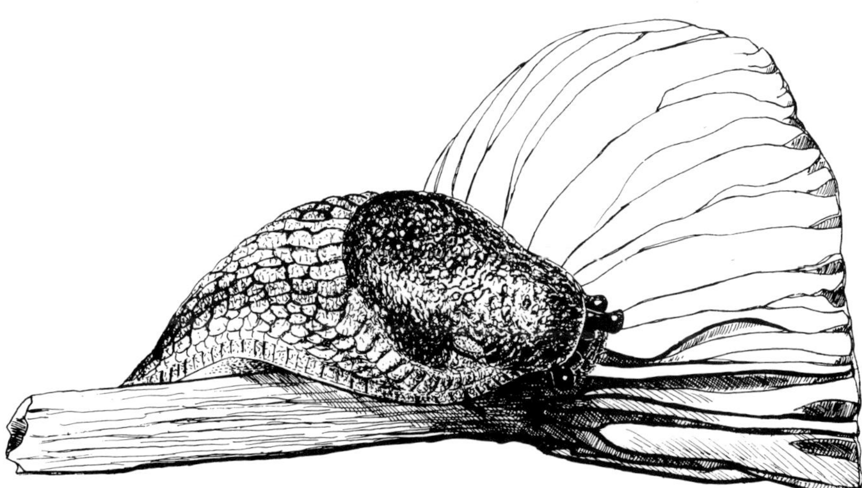

Arion ater

Appendix 14

Reptiles and Amphibia

Three species of reptile and five species of amphibia occur at Shotover. Occasional records of adder *(Vipura berus)* have been received but as there is a possibility of confusion with grass snake, they should perhaps be regarded as doubtful. All three species of newt have been seen in the Henry Stephen/C.S. Lewis pond. The nationally rare crested newt is not uncommon in ponds near Oxford.

REPTILES
Natrix natrix   Grass snake   **1,8,13**
Lacerta vivipera   Common lizard   **1,8,13**
Anguis fragilis   Slow worm   **1,8**
AMPHIBIA
Rana temporaria   Frog   **1,8,13**
Bufo bufo   Toad   **1,13**
Triturus helveticus   Palmated newt   **13**
T. vulgaris   Smooth newt   **13**
T. cristatus   Crested newt   **13**

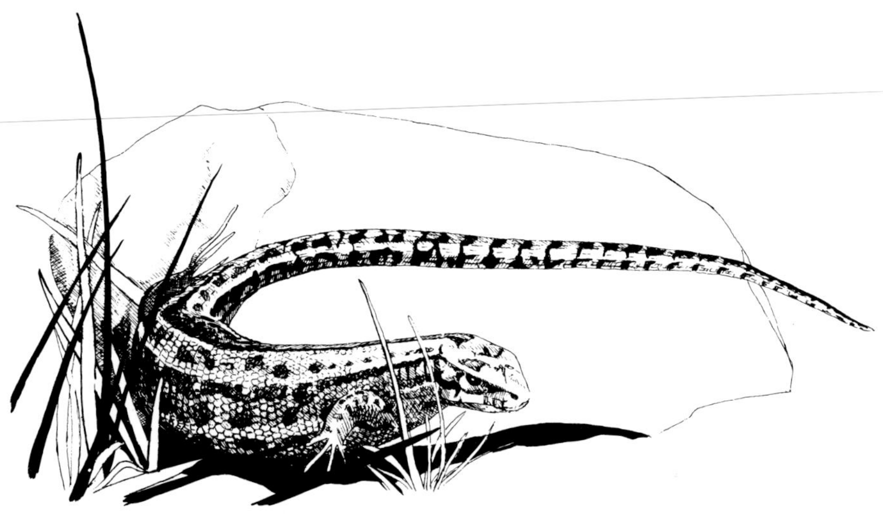

   Common lizard (Lacerta vivipara)

Birds

Although no unusual birds nest at Shotover any longer, substantial numbers of common birds breed there. Woodland is a particularly important habitat for breeding birds because it supports a much greater density of birds than other habitats. There has been a noticeable decline in such heathland species as nightjar, wheatear, whinchat and stonechat due in part to the scrubbing over of suitable habitat. If the heathland were restored it is by no means certain that these birds would return to breed, but it is possible that at least some would return over a period of years.

Little grebe *Tachybaptus ruficollis*   Little grebes breed in small numbers on some of Shotover's large ponds. Their loud, whinnying calls make them easy to locate in the breeding season. Little grebes are carnivorous, feeding on small fish.

Grey heron *Ardea cinerea*   Herons are often seen flying over Shotover but as the nearest heronry is some miles away Shotover must be on a regularly used flight path.

Mallard *Anas platyrhyncos*   Mallards breed on some of Shotover's larger ponds and occasionally roost on even the smallest ponds.

Buzzard *Buteo buteo*   Buzzards are occasionally seen overhead in late summer. They nest in one or two sites in the extreme south and west of Oxfordshire but there are no breeding records for Shotover.

Rough-legged buzzard *Buteo lagopus*   A single record (14 October 1973) exists for this uncommon visitor to Britain.

Sparrowhawk *Accipiter nisus*   Although they usually nest in conifers, sparrowhawks are now so common in the county that they nest in oaks at Shotover. They feed mainly on smaller birds. Between 1955 and 1965 the numbers of sparrowhawks in Britain crashed dramatically. This crash was connected to the increased use in agriculture of toxic chemical sprays and in particular chlorinated hydro-carbons. The early 1980s have seen an equally dramatic increase in sparrowhawk numbers in Oxfordshire following the decreased use of these chemicals.

Hen Harrier *Circus cyaneus*   Last recorded at Shotover on 24 January 1921, hen harriers are regularly seen near Oxford in winter. 200 years ago hen harriers bred in Southern England but their numbers fell dramatically in the early 1900s and for a while they bred only in the Orkneys.

Hobby *Falco subbuteo*   This attractive falcon is a summer visitor from Africa and it is only present in its restricted breeding area for 5 months of the year. These birds are the last of the summer migrants to be seen at Shotover where, although they do not nest, they may occasionally be seen on their extended hunting trips searching for large insects and hirundines.

Kestrel *Falco tinnunculus*   The kestrel is the bird of prey most likely to be seen at Shotover and several pairs nest locally. Kestrels feed mainly on rodents, short-tailed voles in particular, and they will often be seen quartering the ground and hovering in search of prey.

Partridge *Perdix perdix*   The native grey partridge may occasionally be seen in the fields and open woods on the lower slopes of the hill, where breeding probably occurs but has not been proven.

Red-legged partridge *Alectoris rufa*   Introduced in the nineteenth century, red-legged partridges are now commoner than grey partridges at Shotover.

Pheasant *Phasianus colchicus*   Pheasants were probably introduced to England by the Normans in the eleventh century and became widespread by the sixteenth century. There are several active pheasant shoots near Oxford where birds are reared in large numbers for sport – Woodeaton, Long and Noke Woods are all used for pheasant rearing.

Water rail *Rallus aquaticus*   This skulking bird has been seen in dense aquatic vegetation at Shotover, but breeding has not been proven.

Moorhen *Gallinula chloropus*   Moorhens are the commonest breeding waterbirds at Shotover. These familiar birds nest near almost all of Shotover's ponds.

Coot *Fulica atra*   Coots are a familiar feature of Shotover's larger ponds and small lakes. These conspicuous birds dive to take beakfuls of vegetation from the floor of the pond before returning to the surface to eat.

Snipe *Gallinago gallinago*   The harsh December of 1981 saw a snipe feeding on Brasenose pond for about one week.

Woodcock *Scolopax rusticola*   This beautiful wader is not known to breed at Shotover, probably because there is not a sufficiently extensive tract of woodland. However, woodcock are regularly seen in woodland when they stop off on winter migration.

Lesser black-backed gull *Larus fuscus* and **herring gull** *L. argentatus*   These gulls are often seen overhead and following the plough on the lower slopes of the hill.

Black-headed gulls *L. ridibundus* are rarely seen overhead.

Feral pigeon *Columba livia*   Feral pigeons are closely related to the wild rock doves which are now only found in West Scotland and Ireland. Feral pigeons are semi-domesticated birds which until the time of the Napoleonic Wars were an important element of the rural economy. These birds nest in outbuildings at Shotover and are frequently seen feeding on arable fields nearby.

Wood pigeon *Columba palumbus*   Wood pigeons are serious agricultural pests which consume large quantities of grain. They breed in abundance at Shotover, and their white wing-bars and wing-clapping display flights are frequently seen.

Stock dove *Columba oenas*   Stock doves nest in tree holes, unlike the other British pigeons and doves. Their far-carrying but soft song and their display flights make these doves easy to locate.

Turtle dove *Streptopelia turtur*   The purring song of this migrant dove is reminiscent of high summer. One or two pairs nest in the scrub of Shotover's hillside but the numbers are less than might be expected. This probably reflects the shortage of weed seeds, the staple food of the turtle dove, in the agricultural fields nearby.

Collared dove *Streptopelia decaocto*   This handsome dove has only bred in this country since 1955 and in this county since 1962, but it has increased in numbers since then. Collared doves feed mainly on grain and other seeds and they may be seen feeding in allotments and large, private gardens at Shotover.

Cuckoo *Cuculus canorus*   The strange breeding habits of this species are well known but it is less well known that females lay from 12-25 eggs per season, each in a different nest. Dunnock and robin are probably the commonest hosts at Shotover. Cuckoos are becoming scarcer over the country as a whole and nowadays they are rarely seen in woodland.

Barn owl *Tyto alba*   This beautiful owl has not been seen at Shotover in recent years although breeding was suspected on the north side of the hill in 1961. Indeed barn owls have become scarce near Oxford over the past five years with many birds disappearing from established territories.

Little owl *Athene noctua*   Not indigenous to Britain, little owls were initially released in Kent in the 1870s and in other parts of the country in succeeding years. These small owls nest in tree holes in hedgerow oaks and elms on the lower slopes of the hill. They feed on a wide variety of animal life including small mammals, birds and insects and have been seen following the plough at Shotover.

Tawny owl *Strix aluco*   Several pairs of tawny owls breed at Shotover, nesting in tree holes. Newly emerged owlets may be seen sitting together on a branch near the nest hole in April and May. The well known hooting of this species may be heard at night throughout the autumn and winter.

Nightjar *Caprimulgus europaeus*   Typically a bird of dry, sandy heaths, there has been a widespread and drastic decline in nightjar numbers since the end of the nineteenth century. This decline is still progressing and so, although a nightjar was recorded at Shotover in 1936, it is unlikely that they will return in the near future.

Swift *Apus apus*   Although they are not known to breed on the hillside, parties of screaming swifts are a common and familiar sight in summer as they feed on insects high over Shotover.

Kingfisher *Alcedo atthis*   The vividly coloured kingfisher is occasionally seen in Shotover Spinney and Sydling's Copse.

Green woodpecker *Picus viridis*   3-4 pairs nest on Shotover Hill and such a high density suggests that the habitat is very suitable with a combination of mature oaks for nesting and open ground for insect feeding. It is a very noisy bird and its loud, laughing cry gives rise to its country name of "yaffle".

Great spotted woodpecker *Dendrocopos major*   Great spotted woodpeckers are most likely to be seen in the vicinity of mature trees because they feed on bark insects. A loud drumming noise, produced by repeatedly hammering the beak against wood, is their substitute for a territorial song. Several pairs of these attractive woodpeckers nest at Shotover although the felling of the last dead elm trees reduced their food supply.

Lesser spotted woodpeckers *Dendrocopos minor*   These sparrow-sized woodpeckers are much less common than the other two species. A single pair is often seen in Brasenose Wood and Johnson's Piece and occasionally in the other Shotover woods.

Woodlark *Lullula arborea*   Woodlarks bred near Shotover Plain from 1949-1956. Since the 1950s there has been a rapid contraction of the woodlark's range in Britain. The possible reasons for this are the shortage of close cropped grass following the results of myxomatosis and the preponderance of cool, wet summers in the 1950s and 1960s.

Skylark *Alauda arvensis*   The skylark is the most widely distributed of British birds but few pairs nest at Shotover.

Swallow *Hirundo rustica*   The arrival of the swallow early in April is a herald of spring. Their nests are almost always attached to man-made structures and they are one of the species that are far more abundant now than in the days before man.

House martin *Delichon urbica*   These attractive little martins are frequently seen feeding with swallows at Shotover, but although many apparently suitable house eaves are available none have been seen nesting.

Carrion crow *Corvus corone*   The crow's solitary nest perched high in oak trees is a common sight at Shotover. They feed on a wide variety of animal matter including eggs and young nestling birds.

Rook *Corvus frugilegus*   These noisy, gregarious birds were common near Open Brasenose until 1978 when their elm-tree homes werre felled, having succumbed to Dutch Elm disease. Since then they are seen much less often and there is no rookery on the hillside.

Jackdaw *Corvus monedula*   These largely insectivorous birds with their conspicuous grey napes are abundant at Shotover breeding both in tree holes and in chimneys.

Magpie *Pica pica*   Between 10 and 15 pairs of magpies nest in the thorn bushes of Shotover and flocks of up to 15 birds may be seen feeding on open ground. During the nineteenth and early twentieth centuries magpies suffered greatly from keepering because, although they feed mainly on invertebrates and berries, they do occasionally take eggs and young birds.

Jay *Garrulus glandarius*   This large, brightly coloured bird is common in coppice-with-standards woodland in Britain. 3-4 pairs nest in Brasenose Wood and it is thought that these birds help to propagate oaks by burying acorns.

Great tit *Parus major*   The loud, ringing "tee-cha" song of the great tit is a common and unmistakable sound at Shotover. These rather quarrelsome tits nest in tree holes and often feed on the ground.

Blue tit *Parus caeruleus*   Blue tits are abundant at Shotover. The large number of mature oaks provide ideal conditions both in terms of invertebrate food and nesting holes.

Coal tit *Parus ater*   The song of these small tits may be confused with that of the great tit but the smaller size and the white nape are distinctive. Although coal tits are more numerous in the vicinity of Shotover's conifers, feeding on insects amongst the needles, they do nest in the exclusively deciduous Brasenose Wood.

Marsh tit *Parus palustris*   Several pairs of marsh tits breed at Shotover and silver birches are often chosen for nesting. These noisy birds sing loudly in early spring and their "pitchou" calls ring throughout the woods.

Willow tit *Parus montanus*   Willow tits look very similar to marsh tits and the small morphological differences are difficult to pick out in the field. Willow tits excavate their own nest holes, unlike marsh tits, and consequently chips of wood will be found under the nest. The willow tit is much quieter than the marsh tit, its piping song is rarely heard, but it does produce a distinctive nasal buzzing sound. Fewer willow than marsh tits breed at Shotover.

Long-tailed tit *Aegithalos caudatos*   Unlike tits of the genus *Parus* the long-tailed tit builds a nest in a bush consisting of moss, cobwebs, hair, lichen and feathers. These beautiful birds have unusual breeding behaviour and often several birds attend a single nest.

Nuthatch *Sitta europaea*   These noisy, rather quarrelsome birds may be heard singing throughout the spring in some of Shotover's woodlands. They feed on bark insects and nuts, and penetrate acorns by wedging them in tree bark and then using their powerful bills to break the shells. The remains of these nuts may be found in the ridged oak bark.

Treecreeper *Certhia familiaris*   Like the previous species the treecreeper spends most of its time looking for insects on tree bark. Being small and drably coloured and having a rather thin song, they are not often seen but are more numerous than nuthatches at Shotover.

Wren *Troglodytes troglodytes*   The loud, vehement song of the wren may be heard from early spring until the end of the summer and is a familiar sound at Shotover. Like all small birds, wrens suffer greatly in cold winters but the recent succession of mild winters has allowed them to increase in numbers.

Mistle thrush *Turdus viscivorus*   The loud fluted song of the mistle thrush, uttered from a high perch, may be heard from late December until June. They are one of the earliest species to lay and they usually have a second brood.

Fieldfare *Turdus pilaris*   Fieldfares are winter visitors and their harsh flight calls are frequently heard over Shotover. They feed in small flocks on open fields on the lower slopes. Fieldfares breed in Scandinavia and the Baltic region but their range is extending westward.

Song thrush *Turdus philomelos*   This common bird has a well known song which includes many repeated phrases which assist recognition. At Shotover song thrushes are about as common as the related mistle thrush, but over the country as a whole song thrushes are by far the more numerous.

Redwing *Turdus iliacus*   Redwings are winter visitors to Oxfordshire. They nest in Scandinavia and in recent years they have started to breed in Scotland in small numbers. At Shotover, flocks of redwings may be seen feeding on haws or rustling in leaf litter looking for invertebrate food.

Blackbird *Turdus merula*   One of our most familiar birds, blackbirds are abundant at Shotover. Their beautiful, melodic song is best heard early in the morning and at dusk, and their churring alarm call is often heard during the daytime.

Wheatear *Oenanthe oenanthe*   Wheatears are typically birds of remote uplands but a few pairs breed in Southern England in areas where grazing by sheep and rabbit maintains a short sward. A report in the 1931 bulletin of the Oxford Ornithological Society states that "... many years ago Wheatears bred at Shotover but they have long since ceased to do so." This report suggests that Shotover was once rather more of a remote upland than it is today. Wheatears are still seen occasionally on brief stop-overs on spring and autumn passage.

Stonechat *Saxicola torquata*   Stonechats breed in rough country with gorse, heather or bracken and close-cropped grass. Stonechats bred at Shotover in 1889, 1935 and 1936 but there has been no nesting in recent years. Few inland

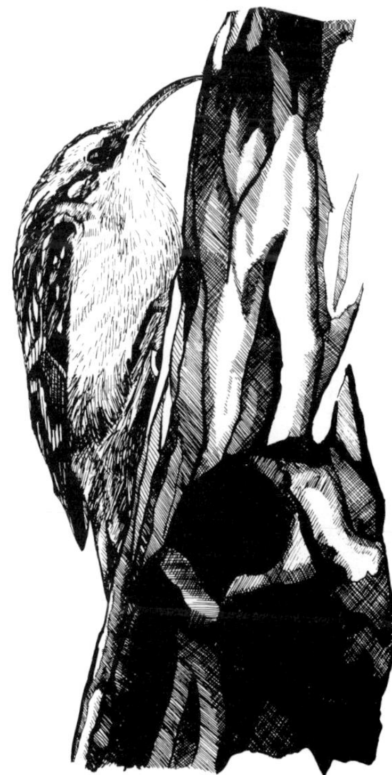

Treecreeper (Certhia familiaris)

heaths support many stonechats but they are occasionally seen at Shotover during the winter months.

Whinchat *Saxicola rubetra*   Whinchats are heathland birds which are more common on inland heaths than the related stonechats. Whinchats bred regularly at Shotover until 1958 and we must assume that their departure was caused by the diminution of their heathland habitat.

Redstart *Phoenicurus phoenicurus*   Redstarts are uncommon breeding birds in Oxfordshire, although these attractive summer visitors are abundant in parts of Scotland and Wales. Redstarts were recorded at Shotover in 1939 and 1952.

Nightingale *Luscinia megarhynchos*   The magnificent song of the nightingale may be heard in some years at Shotover but in other years it is absent. Nightingales were recorded in 1934, 1937, 1943, 1945, 1947, 1948, 1950, 1952, 1955, 1965 and 1978 but they were absent in 1975, 1976, 1977, 1979 and 1982. The population of nightingales in Britain is declining and as Oxford is near the north west limit of their breeding range it is not too surprising that their occurrence is sporadic. A recent study[61] has shown that a rich and constantly changing ground flora is a common component of nightingale territories, and this is most likely to occur where coppice-with-standards is being actively managed. Optimum habitat occurs when the coppice is 5-8 years old. It is likely that the decline in nightingale numbers is caused by a decrease in coppicing.

Robin *Erithacus rubecula*   This, the best known and most loved of British birds, is abundant at Shotover. Their song may be heard throughout the year but at about the time that the young are fledged the song changes and becomes more melancholic, as if mourning the passing of spring.

Grasshopper warbler *Locustella naevia*   Grasshopper warblers depend on thick, low, tangled vegetation for nesting and their distinctive, reeling song may be heard at a distance of up to 1 km. They breed in small numbers at two places on the lower slopes of the hill.

Reed warbler *Acrocephalus scirpaceus*   Reed warblers require extensive reed beds for nesting and the Shotover area has very little suitable habitat. However, they have been heard singing from time to time and may breed sporadically near Shotover House.

Sedge warbler *Acrocephalus schoenobaenus*   A few areas of reeds and luxuriant waterside vegetation at Shotover support a small number of sedge warblers. Their rattling, far-carrying song may be heard from April until mid-July.

Blackcap *Sylvia atricapilla*   The rich and beautiful song of the blackcap rivals that of the nightingale and blackbird, and like the latter is usually uttered from a high perch. In recent years there has been a trend for some blackcaps to overwinter in Britain and some have been seen visiting bird tables near Shotover. Ringing studies have shown that these winter blackcaps are eastern European birds which migrate here in October and November. Unlike most warblers blackcaps will take fruit if insects are in short supply and it is probably this adaptability which enables them to survive our winter.

Garden warbler *Sylvia borin*   The song of the garden warbler is similar to that of the blackcap and the two are often difficult to distinguish. Garden warblers were much scarcer than blackcaps at Shotover in the period 1975-1983 but in 1927 they were reported to be "remarkably numerous" in Johnson's Piece.

Whitethroat *Sylvia communis*   Several pairs of white-throat nest at Shotover. They choose a thorn thicket for nesting and the presence of nearby open grassland seems to be desirable.

Lesser whitethroat *Sylvia curruca*   This skulking bird nests in thick scrub and Shotover provides a good deal of suitable habitat. The lesser whitethroat's presence is confirmed by its distinctive but unmelodic, rattling song which is reminiscent of the first part of the chaffinch's song.

Willow warbler *Phylloscopus trochilus*   With their familiar descending trill of silvery notes the willow warbler is a welcome spring arrival to Shotover. In 1959 it was estimated that there were 100 pairs and the population has changed little since then.

Chiffchaff *Phylloscopus collybita*   The reiterated song notes of the chiffchaff are penetrating and heard all over the hillside during spring. The chiffchaff, like most other warblers, is cryptically coloured to avoid predation, but to ensure that a mate is found has a loud and penetrating song.

Wood warbler *Phylloscopus sibilatrix*   Wood warblers are strictly confined to mature, deciduous woodland. They are uncommon breeders in Oxfordshire but they do nest sporadically at Shotover, being recorded in 1945, 1949, 1971, 1972 and 1975. In 1979 a male sang in Brasenose Wood but it did not breed.

Goldcrest *Regulus regulus*   This tiny bird nests in small numbers in Shotover's conifers but may be seen feeding in deciduous trees.

Firecrest *Regulus ignicapillus*   Firecrests were first known to have bred in England in 1962 and since then their range has expanded. As their song, appearance and habitat is similar to that of the goldcrest they are easily overlooked. The first confirmed sight record for Shotover was in a small, young larch plantation near Westhill Farm in spring 1983.

Spotted flycatcher *Muscicapa striata*   Spotted fly-catchers are one of the last summer migrants to arrive. They have a dull plumage and a thin song but the aerobatic forays for food quickly reveal the flycatcher's presence.

Pied flycatcher *Ficedula hypoleuca*   Pied flycatchers, which breed in north and west Britain, have been heard singing twice at Shotover (1981, 1983) for short periods.

Dunnock *Prunella modularis*   Dunnocks are abundant at Shotover and although they are visually inconspicuous, may be easily recognised by their fast, rather squeaky song.

Tree pipit *Anthus trivialis*   In recent years tree pipits have become scarce as breeding birds in Oxfordshire. They were recorded at Shotover in 1934, 1951, 1958 and 1960 (4 pairs) but they had disappeared by 1962. Breeding had ceased in Sydling's Copse by the mid 1970s. In 1979 a male was seen performing its characteristic aerobatic display in Slade Camp north but it did not breed.

Pied wagtail *Motacilla alba*   Pied wagtails are not often seen at Shotover because of the preponderance of woodland and scrub and lack of more suitable wet habitats. However, a few pairs breed regularly near to freshwater.

Grey wagtail *Motacilla cinerea*   Grey wagtails breed near freshwater streams and rivers. A pair has been seen on several occasions in the vicinity of the ponds in Shotover Spinney but breeding has not been confirmed.

Red-backed shrike *Lanius collurio*   Red-backed shrikes have been declining in range and number in Britain for over 100 years and they are now extremely scarce breeders. Red-backed shrikes bred in Johnson's Piece in 1930 and in Open Brasenose in 1944 but have not been recorded since.

Starling *Sturnus vulgaris*   Starlings are abundant at Shotover nesting in large numbers in both tree holes and

Birds

outbuildings. These familiar birds have a disarming ability to mimic other bird songs, such a the green woodpecker, and even sounds such as the screeching of car brakes.

Hawfinch *Coccothraustes coccothraustes*   This large, heavy-billed finch is extremely elusive as it is shy, does not have a distinctive song and spends its time high in the deciduous tree canopy. It was recorded at Shotover in 1927, 1936 and 1937.

Greenfinch *Carduelis chloris*   Greenfinches nest in small numbers in the scrub at Shotover but they are more numerous in peripheral gardens where they frequently visit bird tables. Their bat-like display flight and characteristic nasal "dszwee" call make greenfinches easily recognized.

Goldfinch *Carduelis carduelis*   Goldfinches feed on weed seed and in autumn they are fond of thistle and knapweed seed-heads. They have a characteristic twittering flight call which resembles that of a linnet, but their brightly coloured plumage is quite distinctive.

Siskin *Carduelis spinus*   Siskins breed in the conifer forests of Northern Scotland but they are occasionally seen feeding in mature conifers at Shotover. They are usually to be seen in flocks of redpolls with which they may be confused.

Linnet *Acanthis cannabina*   Linnets feed on weed seeds and so are usually to be found in small colonies in gardens on the periphery of Shotover and in particular on allotments. Their cheerful, twittering song is especially welcome in summer when birdsong is at a premium.

Redpoll *Acanthis flammea*   Small flocks of redpolls are regularly seen at Shotover, both in mature conifers and in deciduous woodland, but breeding has not been confirmed.

Bullfinch *Pyrrhula pyrrhula*   Shotover's blackthorn scrub provides ideal nesting sites for this attractive finch. Bullfinches are serious pests in some places because of their habit of eating fruit blossom buds, but they cause no problems in their natural woodland edge habitat.

Crossbill *Loxia curvirosta*   The crossbill's specially adapted beak, with the tips of the hooked mandibles overlapping, enables it to extract seeds from cones. Crossbills breed in Northern Scotland and a few scattered southerly localities, but occasionally great numbers of immigrants are seen in this country. When these irruptions occur birds are usually seen at Shotover and flocks were recorded in 1929, 1936 and 1963.

Chaffinch *Fringilla coelebs*   The widespread and abundant chaffinch breeds in woodland and scrub at Shotover having spent most of the winter in fields around the hill. Its cheerful, rollicking call with a distinctive final flourish is a welcome addition to the woods in spring.

Brambling *Fringilla montifringilla*   Bramblings do not breed in this country but are winter visitors. They resemble the related chaffinch in many ways but have a prominent white rump. Bramblings are seen in small numbers at Shotover each winter.

Corn bunting *Emberiza calandra*   Corn buntings have been heard singing from hedgerows in arable fields below Shotover and breeding is probable. An interesting feature of the breeding biology of this species is that an individual male supports several females.

Yellowhammer *Emberiza citrinella*   The gorse of Shotover Hill and the hedgerows of the lower fields provide nesting sites for this familiar and attractive bunting. Their well-known "little-bit-of-bread-and-no-cheese" song may be heard from February until August.

Reed bunting *Emberiza schoeniclus*   These pretty, black-headed buntings are occasionally seen feeding at Shotover and they breed in some of the wet areas.

House sparrow *Passer domesticus*   House sparrows are commensal with man and are found breeding in large numbers in most of Oxfordshire's buildings. Although rarely seen away from domestication, they do feed in small flocks in the woods when insect food is abundant.

Tree sparrow *Passer montanus*   Similar to the house sparrow except for its chestnut head, tree sparrows are easily overlooked. Breeding was reported at Shotover in 1960, 1962 and 1965 but has not been confirmed in recent years.

Nomenclature after Sharrock, J.T.R. (1977) The Atlas of Breeding Birds in Britain and Ireland. T. & A.D. Poyser.

Linnet (Acanthis cannabina)

Appendix 16

Mammals

Hedgehog *Erinaceus europaeus*   This unmistakable animal is regularly seen in the gardens surrounding Shotover, and as a road casualty. Hedgehogs are entirely nocturnal which accounts for the comparatively few sightings.

Mole *Talpa europaea*   Fresh mole-hills, which are recently excavated soil from the mole's underground burrows, are a common sight over Shotover Hill and the surrounding woodlands.

Common shrew *Sorex araneus*   Shrews are active throughout the day and night and take a wide range of invertebrates, with beetles and earthworms forming a major part of their diet. They are found throughout Shotover and are frequently killed by domestic cats.

Pygmy shrew *Sorex minutus*   Pygmy shrews are difficult to distinguish from common shrews but they are slightly smaller in size, have a proportionately longer tail and a more uniform colouration.

Water shrew *Neomys fodiens*   Water shrews may be recognised by their black upper parts and by the red tips to their teeth. They have been taken from the Slade Camp north and are not as dependent on water as their name suggests.

Bats *(Chiroptera)*   The most spectacular behavioural characteristic of bats is undoubtedly their development of sonar. Most British bats find their way predominantly by echolocation, emitting high-pitched sounds at about 80,000 cycles per second and interpreting the reflected soundwaves to distinguish between obstacles to flight and prey. Bats present problems of identification and they need to be hand held for positive determination. Many bats have been seen at Shotover but the only species which has been identified with reasonable certainty is the pipistrelle (*Pipistrellum pipist, ellum*) which is a small bat seen flying at dusk. Bats larger than pipistrelles have been seen which may be noctules (*Nyctalus noctula*).

Rabbit *Oryctolagus cuniculus*   Rabbits were introduced to Britain in the twelfth century for their meat and fur but did not become widely established until much later. The Shotover rabbit population was decimated in 1954 by the arrival of myxomatosis a viral disease transmitted by the rabbit flea. At Shotover the number of rabbits present remains very variable and the observed population crashes may still be connected with myxomatosis. Rabbits have an important influence on vegetation. Their close grazing maintains a short sward which favours fine-leaved grasses and prevents the establishment of scrub. Many scrub thickets can be dated to the early 1950s and can therefore be directly attributed to the onset of myxomatosis.

Hare *Lepus capensis*   Hares have been declining in Oxfordshire in recent years. At Shotover they are scarce and are only found in the fields close to Stowood and Sydling's Copse. Shallow depressions where they lie up may be found in rough grassland and the woodland edge.

Grey squirrel *Sciurus carolinensis*   Grey squirrels were introduced to Britain from U.S.A. in 1876 and were introduced to Oxfordshire between 1890 and 1905. Grey squirrels are abundant in woodland at Shotover where they feed on tree mast, seeds, leaves and fungi. They also take bark from young trees which causes die-back and distorted growth, and for this reason are regarded by many as pests.

Harvest mouse (Micromys minutus)

Mammals

Red squirrel *Sciurus vulgaris*   Prior to the introduction of the grey squirrel, red squirrels were common in Oxfordshire but their numbers declined dramatically between 1910 and 1925. An endemic virus carried by the grey squirrel has been postulated as the cause of the red squirrel's demise. However, marked fluctuations in the numbers of red squirrel were observed prior to the introduction of the grey squirrel, and it may be that the main influence of the latter is to prevent recolonization of the native red squirrel.

Bank vole *Clethrionomys glareolus*   Bank voles are abundant in Shotover's woodland where they feed on fruits, seeds and leaves. They feed during the daytime and so are more likely to be seen than mice or shrews, from which they may be distinguished by their blunter muzzles.

Field vole *Microtus agrestis*   One of the commonest and most widespread of British rodents, field voles are abundant in grassland at Shotover. Like the bank vole they are active throughout the 24 hours and so may be seen during the daytime.

Wood mouse *Apodemus sylvaticus*   The wood mouse is the characteristic rodent of deciduous woodland living in small runways beneath the litter. Wood mice are nocturnal and so are not often seen.

Harvest mouse *Micromys minutus*   The harvest mouse is the smallest British rodent weighing only 6 grams when adult. They are easily distinguished by their size, their small, hairy ears and blunt muzzle. Harvest mice have been seen on the periphery of Brasenose Wood but probably occur over much of Shotover. Their nests may be found in the stalks of vegetation well above ground level.

House mouse *Mus musculus*   House mice are not easy to distinguish from wood mice but they have a greyer-brown colouration and a characteristic 'stale' smell not found in wood mice. They have been found in Britain since the Iron Age but it is thought that they are not truly native. They are abundant in the houses and outbuildings at Shotover and are found in smaller numbers away from habitation.

Common rat *Rattus norvegicus*   The common rat is thought to have been introduced to Britain in the early years of the eighteenth century when it replaced the ship rat (*R. rattus*) which had been present for hundreds of years. Rats are an important vector of human disease. At Shotover they are associated with large gardens and domestic animals.

Fox *Vulpes vulpes*   The familiar fox is common at Shotover but because of its nocturnal habits is not often seen. Foxes are opportunists which regularly scavenge in suburban housing estates, such as Wood Farm and Headington Quarry, but they prefer woodland for their earths. Foxes are predators and scavengers and as such have an important function in the natural community. The fox's mating season is January and February and vixens may be heard screaming at this time. This screaming is an eerie and rather frightening noise reminiscent of a child crying.

Stoat *Mustela erminea*   Stoats are larger than the closely related weasels and may be recognised with certainty by the black tip to their tail. Stoats are efficient predators able to take prey as large as rabbits, although they also take birds and small rodents. Since myxomatosis the stoat population has declined dramatically and they are rarely seen at Shotover.

Weasel *Mustela nivalis*   Weasels are much more common than stoats at Shotover. Weasels feed primarily on small rodents, bank voles in particular, but they also take small birds. Family parties of weasels are occasionally seen in May, with the young following a parent in a line.

Badger *Meles meles*   For such a large animal badgers are rarely seen, feeding only at night and spending the daylight hours in their sets. There are five known sets at Shotover but a careful search might well reveal more. Badger's prints, which are easily distinguished from other mammals, show that they forage a long way from their sets.

Feral cat *Felis sp.*   Cats of domestic origin living in the wild are an underrated source of predation on rodents and small birds. Although there are no packs of feral cats at Shotover several individuals have been seen.

Fallow deer *Dama dama*   Fallow deer were probably introduced to Britain by the Normans but remains have been found from the last interglacial period. These large deer are common in extensive areas of woodland near Oxford, such as Wytham Woods and Bernwood Forest, but at Shotover they are only seen regularly in Holly and Stanton Great Woods.

Roe deer *Capreolus capreolus*   Roe deer became virtually extinct in England by the beginning of the eighteenth century and the present population in South England is the result of later introductions. Roe deer were certainly present at Shotover in medieval times. There has been one recent doubtful sighting at Shotover but as roe deer are extending their range from strongholds in Surrey and Sussex, it will be interesting to see whether they eventually return to Oxfordshire.

Muntjac *Muntiacus reevesi*   Muntjac are the commonest deer at Shotover. They are easily recognised by their small size, rounded back and the males by their tusks and simple antlers. Asian in origin, muntjac escaped from Woburn deer park in about 1900. Muntjac are also called barking deer because of their habit of making loud, barking noises in the rutting season.

Nomenclature after Corbet, G.B. and Southern, H.N. (1977). A Handbook of British Mammals. 2nd ed. Blackwells.

Bibliography

1 Morris, J. (1978) *Domesday book, text and translation.* Oxfordshire. Philimore.
2 Hassall, W.O. (1956), *Wheatley Records.* Cheney & Sons.
3 *Oxfordshire Victoria County History*, Vol. 1. University of London Institute of Historical Research.
4 Watney, V.J. (1910) *Cornbury and the Forest of Wychwood.* Hatchards.
5 *Berks, Bucks and Oxon Archaeological Journal* IV, 27 (1898)
6 Young, C.J. (1977) Oxfordshire Roman Pottery, *British Archaeological Reports*, 43.
7 *Boarstall Cartulary* (1930) O.H.S.
8 Roberts, E. (1963) The boundary and woodlands of Shotover Forest c.1298, *Oxoniensia* 28, 68 – 73.
9 Whiting, J. (1643) True description, measurement and survey of Shottover Forest, Ref. no. 355. P.R.O.
10 Cal. Lib. 1245 – 51, 333.
11 Cox, J.C. (1905) *The Royal Forests of England.* Methuen and Co.
12 *Oxfordshire Victoria County History.* Vol. 5. University of London Institute of Historical Research.
13 MS Top Oxon S117 f33.
14 Cal. Pat. 1301 – 7, 333.
15 Plot, R. (1677) *A Natural History of Oxfordshire.*
16 Macray, W.D. (1894 – 1915). *Register of Magdalen College, Oxford.*
17 Wood, A. (1894) *The Life and Times of Antony Wood*, Vol. 3. O.H.S.
18 Langdon, T. (1605) *The description of a tenement and certain parcels of pasture meadow and wood ground in Horspath . . . belonging to Corpus Christi College.*
19 B.N.C. Valuation Book 3, 89.
20 Dunkin, D. (1935) *Oxoniensia* ii, 439.
21 Wood, A. (1979) *Oxford Mail* 28.ix.79.
22 Aubrey (undated MS) *Monumenta Brittanica*
23 6″ – 1 mile aerial photograph taken by R.A.F. August 1947. Ordnance Survey Office.
24 Fairfax E. (undated) *Calling All Arms.* Hutchinson & Co. Ltd.
25 B.N.C. correspondence, 878.
26 Druce, G.C. (1886) *Flora of Oxfordshire*, ed. 1. Parker & Co.
27 Druce, G.C. (1927) *Flora of Oxfordshire*, ed. 2. Clarendon Press.
28 Jones, E.W. (1953) A bryophyte flora of Berkshire and Oxfordshire. I. Hepaticae *Trans. Brit. Bryol. Soc.* 2, 19 – 32.
29 Jones, E.W. (1953) A bryophyte flora of Berkshire and Oxfordshire. II. Musci *Trans. Brit. Bryol. Soc.* 2, 220 – 277.
30 Goode, D. (1981) *The threat to wildlife habitats.* New Scientist 22.1.81.
31 Hobson, M.G. and Price, K.L.H. (1961) *Otmoor and its seven towns.*
32 Pollard, E., Hooper, M. and Moore, N. (1974) *Hedges.* New Naturalist, Collins.
33 Forest Hill Women's Institute Year Book, 1933.
34 Calendar of Charter Rolls (1906) 1257 – 1300. P.R.O. London
35 Gelling, M. (1953) *The place names of Oxfordshire.* English Place Names Society. XXIII. Cambridge.
36 B.N.C. Archives, 16 Estates (1).
37 Brasenose Quartercentenary Monographs (1909) vi, 19.
38 B.N.C. Archives, 16 Estates (3).
39 B.N.C. Archives, 16, Estates (24).
40 The book of accounts for the new buildings in Oxford (1656), 43.
41 B.N.C. Valuation Book 3, 89.
42 Davis, R. (1797) A new map of the county of Oxford.
43 B.N.C. Archives, 16 Estates (2).
44 *Oxford Times*, 8 January 1933.
45 B.N.C. Ledger No. 26 (Estates Register), 43.
46 1854 Sale Catalogue.
47 1871 Sale Catalogue.
48 *Oxford University Gazette*, 24.xi.08.
49 Church, A.H. (1922) *Introduction to the plant life of the Oxford District* (1), O.U.P.
50 Salter, H.E. (1915) A cartulary of the hospital of St. John the Baptist. *Ox. Hist. Soc.* LXVIII.
51 Property of Magdalen College, 1872.
52 Magdalen College Estates Book 1715 – 66.
53 Magdalen College Timber Book.
54 M.S. Top Oxon. f26.
55 Magdalen Papers 1892 – 1900 via Morrell, Peel and Gamlen (Solicitors St. Giles)
56 A register of the estates of St. Mary Magdalen College in the University of Oxford, 1926.
57 Journal of Revd. Charles Wesley, M.A.: early journal, 1736 – 39 (1910), 128.
58 Rose, F., Brown, D.H. et al (1976) *Lichenology: progress and problems.* Academic Press.
59 Hawksworth, D.L. and Rose, F. (1970) Qualitative scale for estimating sulphur dioxide air pollution in England and Wales using epiphytic lichens. *Nature* 227, 145.
60 Rackham, O. (1980) *Ancient woodland its history, vegetation and uses in England.* Edward Arnold.
61 Stuttard, P. and Williamson, K. (1971) Habitat requirements of the Nightingale. *Bird Study* 18, 9 – 14.